A PUBLIC SERVICE

A PUBLIC SERVICE

Whistleblowing, Disclosure and Anonymity

TIM SCHWARTZ

O/R

OR Books
New York · London

All rights information: rights@orbooks.com
Visit our website at www.orbooks.com

First printing 2019

Published by OR Books, New York and London

Library of Congress Cataloging-in-Publication Data: A catalog record for this book is available from the Library of Congress.

Typeset by Lapiz Digital Services. Printed by Bookmobile, USA, and CPI, UK.

paperback ISBN 978-1-68219-222-1 • ebook ISBN 978-1-68219-225-2

Table of Contents

TABLE OF CONTENTS

Introduction

In 1965, 28-year-old Peter Buxtun was hired by the U.S. Public Health Service in San Francisco as a venereal disease investigator. Shortly after starting his job, Buxtun began hearing about a little-known, ongoing study on African-American males with syphilis. To Buxtun's ears, this didn't sound right—by the late 1940s, penicillin had been shown to be an effective drug against syphilis. How could there be an ongoing study of people with a disease that had become rare, thanks to a cheap and effective treatment that was discovered 20 years ago?[1]

Though distracted by a return to school and a law degree, Buxtun continued to follow the trail, contacting the Centers for Disease Control and gathering documentation on the under the radar study. He continued to share the story with those around him, but no one he spoke with knew what to do. Was the study illegal? Surely it was unethical, but would it be possible to do anything about it?

Finally, in 1972, Buxtun found a partner who was interested. He sat down with a reporter from the Associated Press and delivered the information he had gathered.[2] On July 26, 1972, the front page of the *New York Times* carried the headline: "Syphilis Victims in U.S. Study Went Untreated for 40 Years." [3] The public was outraged, and this was the start to the end of the federally sponsored Tuskegee Study. A class-action lawsuit was filed against

1

the U.S. government. Congress passed the National Research Act in 1974, leading to the creation of the Office for Human Research Protections.

Though it was a long time coming, President Bill Clinton eventually offered a formal apology to the survivors in 1997: "The United States government did something that was wrong—deeply, profoundly, morally wrong," said Clinton in his speech to survivors. "It is not only in remembering that shameful past that we can make amends and repair our nation, but it is in remembering that past that we can build a better present and a better future." [4] [5]

The shameful story of the Tuskegee study might never have come to light if someone hadn't decided to speak up and disclose information about the deeply racist experiment. Buxtun listened to his internal moral compass and did something about it. And he wasn't alone: Buxtun had a partner who helped him amplify and contextualize the information for the public.

Unethical acts—not just illegal ones—need to be revealed. Society can only evolve when individuals stand up and shine a light on unethical practices. If you see something that doesn't seem right, speak up. Trust your gut.

The past few years saw a wave of revelations as a result of the #MeToo movement and its cascading disclosures by strong individuals who decided to speak up and reveal the truth. Sexual harassment and assault are rampant around the world, and because these individuals brought this to the forefront of our awareness, others have been able to better identify harassment and understand the actions they can take to do something about it. [6] Our thanks are merited to those who have stood up to harassers and organizations that have allowed illegal or immoral behavior to go unchecked, especially to those who didn't have a clear and safe way to report the harassment. Your work is creating new pathways, hopefully making it easier for those who follow in your footsteps.

This book is for those who want to use information to stand up and shine a light on unethical or illegal practices. The goal is to help people prepare for challenging situations that they might face in the future, and to gain a better understanding of their options and the implications. If you see something you think is wrong but don't know how to do anything about it, let this book be your guide. Challenge systemic issues, point out threats to the public, and disclose fraud, waste, and abuse. Do so by safely releasing information. But there is no reason that you need to lose all you've worked for in your life or go through years of mental anguish and stress because someone else did something wrong. Speak up, but be safe about it!

If you do, you will be joining the ranks of those who have spoken up around the world about sexual harassment, corporate fraud, civil rights violations, mistreatment of animals, medical malpractice, bribery schemes, unethical policing, and anything else that wrongdoers want to keep secret.

Of course, there will be challenges. In 2018, the Global Business Ethics Survey found that employees who reported corruption suffered retaliation 44 percent of the time. Combine this with the fact that we are constantly tracked, leaving a digital trail that reveals where we've been, what we've looked at, and with whom we've communicated, and the odds of disclosing information without retaliation or consequences are slim. But we can increase your chances.

In this book, we offer an alternative solution to this quandary: anonymous research and disclosure. By remaining anonymous, you can stay in control of your identity while planning how to best disclose sensitive information, all while limiting how you can be tracked and attacked by those who might want to stop you. We'll show how to be methodical and how to do research before sending a document to the press. Your first instincts may be your worst option.

Chances are that this will be your first and only time disclosing information—blowing the whistle, as it's known. This isn't something that makes a career. If you screw up—and sometimes even if you don't—there will be consequences. Instead of attempting this process alone, you can partner with someone who can help you navigate the legal, technical, and even emotional challenges that you will face. Whom you choose as your partner will depend on your circumstances and goals. It might be a lawyer, a journalist, or someone who works at a public advocacy organization. No matter with whom you decide to work, you should focus on building trust. Do this by being open, by setting and meeting expectations, and by discussing the best ways to work together. By doing this, you will have much better chances of success and reduce the likelihood of retaliation.

Also, stay up to date. Technology is changing all the time, so researching the technological recommendations in this book on your own is critical. Though these are the best practices at the time of this writing, they may not be by the time you are reading this, though many of the general strategies will hopefully still apply. Do your homework.

For instance, before you start searching for things such as "how to disclose information safely" in your favorite online search engine, read the recommendations in this book. A record of that search could be a piece of data that makes it easy to identify you later on. By the time you have finished reading the chapter on anonymous research, you should be ready to learn more on your own. Until that point, stick with the printed words here. Though you may not realize it, the printed word is likely more secure than anything you could learn on your smartphone or computer. If you can, purchase this book anonymously or gift it to a friend anonymously.

If you do choose to disclose information, it will be hard. Realize this before you start.

You almost certainly won't win an award. Nobody is going to make a movie about you. It will be uncomfortable for your personal life. If you're identified, you will likely be retaliated against. But it is the right thing to do. If the information that you have is eating you up inside and you must tell the world, be sure to do it safely. In many cases you need to be willing to win the fight completely anonymously, without even one other person in the world knowing that it was you who pointed out what was wrong.

To those who take on these risks and speak up for the public and the voiceless—thank you. Only through your help exposing unethical and illegal practices can we make the world a better place.

Good luck, and be safe.

Language and Perceptions

I've tried to limit the use of broad labels and generalizations, including "whistleblower," "leaker," or "victim," and instead to describe specific actions performed by individuals. We will primarily use "disclosure" as the term to describe the act of revealing information. Other terms can inadvertently conflate actions with perceived motives and ethics. Is a whistleblower good or bad? Is the leaker doing something illegal? Does the victim have agency of their own? Accordingly, we will skip labels and instead describe the actions performed. As an example, instead of saying "whistleblower Daniel Ellsberg," we might simply say, "Daniel Ellsberg, who released the Pentagon Papers to the *New York Times*."

Shifting perceptions is one of the goals of the #MeToo movement: to stop slut-shaming and to help those who come forward to be heard and to be believed by default. In many parts of the world, women who report sexual harassment and assault are labeled negatively, and many who target them deny their allegations by default. So far, the #MeToo movement has been successful in moving the dial on these defaults, increasing empathy for those who decide to come forward and report harassment or assault. In turn, this makes it more likely that these crimes will be reported and prosecuted.

In the United States, where the legal system has largely failed victims, only "about 2 percent of sexual assault cases see an arrest, and that is because of bias," said New York lawyer Carrie Goldberg in an NPR interview. She has handled multiple high-profile sexual assault cases, including cases for two of the women allegedly targeted by film producer Harvey Weinstein. "Victims are perceived as opportunists from the outset," Goldberg said, "so the historic default has always been to doubt the accuser, and it's just *so* time for that to end."[7 8]

Perceptions of your actions will always be influenced by the words used to describe you by those around you, by the media, by your allies, and by your adversaries. The language used can cast your actions in a positive or negative light, which can make you seem more or less believable. Understanding this ahead of time will allow you to position yourself and to be ready to respond accordingly.

A good example of positioning can be seen in the initial unveiling of revelations by Edward Snowden, the government security contractor who in 2013 released documentation of the National Security Agency's global surveillance programs. With the help of journalist Glenn Greenwald and the filmmaker Laura Poitras, a video interview was released online, positioning the story of the disclosure perfectly. The video starts with Snowden describing his expertise and the positions he held, and then Greenwald says, "There came some point in time when you crossed this line of thinking about being a whistleblower to making the choice to actually become a whistleblower. Walk people through that decision-making process." This lead-in perfectly frames Snowden as a "whistleblower." The video interview allowed Snowden and his journalist partners to frame perceptions of his actions right from the beginning, using specific language to control the narrative.

7

Perceptions of individuals and their actions can also shift over time. Despite the initial framing in Snowden's first interviews, the public still had a hard time classifying him. Was Snowden a whistleblower, a leaker, or a traitor? A national poll conducted three times over six months following the public release of Snowden's documents came back with approximately the same results each time.[9]

On July 10, 2013, a national poll showed 34 percent of respondents categorized Snowden as a traitor, 57 percent as a whistleblower, and 11 percent said they didn't know. Six months later, on January 9, 2014, the same poll was conducted. The same percentage of people still saw him as a traitor, but 2 percent—within the margin of error—had moved from "don't know" to "whistleblower." As time went on, Snowden increasingly found public support and was increasingly seen in a positive light.

By 2013, the citizens of the United States understood that the definition of a whistleblower had a positive connotation. Despite clear support from the public, however, the news media took a longer time to identify Snowden as a whistleblower, perhaps because of the media's traditional emphasis on appearing to be unbiased. Tom Kent, the deputy managing editor and standards editor of the Associated Press at the time, suggested that journalists either use the term "leaker" to describe Snowden, or that they should simply describe the actions Snowden performed, namely that he "exposed or revealed classified information." In the United States, "leaker" has a more neutral connotation than "whistleblower," which has a positive connotation.[10]

This positive connotation wasn't always attached to the term "whistleblower." It was actually given a strategic makeover by

Ralph Nader in the 1970s. At the time, many different words were associated with people who released information: the snitch, the rat, the tattletale, the informant, the leaker, and the whistleblower. After reading *The Tyranny of Words* by Stuart Chase, a book on semantics, Nader decided to try to rehabilitate the term "whistleblower," choosing the most neutral word as the starting point. Alert to the media's influence, Nader realized that "the press liked the word whistleblower," and that, unlike other word choices, reporters could give it "a meaning of moral courage."[11]

In 1971, Nader and Peter Petkas organized a Conference on Professional Responsibility, and subsequently released a report titled "Whistle Blowing." The conference and report encouraged individuals within corporations to speak up for the greater good, lauding them for doing so. The term was finally codified into law with the Military Whistleblower Protection Act in 1988 and the Whistleblower Protection Act in 1989. By that point, the notion of the word "whistleblower" as heroic was cemented into the American psyche.

Outside America, the term caught on in a number of contexts, particularly in Europe. On April 23, 2018, the European Commission proposed a new initiative for whistleblower protection that would span all the EU countries, with the term "whistleblower" used in the proposal.[12] But the word for "whistleblower" differs from country to country, and of course those words have their own history and connotations.

Understanding that the meanings of words vary greatly depending on context is important in determining how your actions might be judged. It is important to be proactive in attaching words with positive connotations to your actions. For example, in French there are many words for whistleblower. *Lanceur d'alerte* is the most popular and direct translation, but there are other related terms: *signalement, alerte professionnelle, alerte éthique, donneur d'alerte*, and *dénonciation* (which has the most negative connotation). Some countries, such as Finland, seem to only have one word that fits the context: *ilmiantaja*. The connotation of this word is negative. A number of Finns I spoke with used the word "traitor" to translate this word into English, which is clearly not a good thing to be called. The Netherlands, on the other hand, has the word *klokkenluider*, which translates as "bell ringer," evoking the idea of someone ringing the church bell to warn the town of danger. Being a whistleblower in Finland might be more challenging than in the Netherlands, given the associations with the respective country's vocabulary for "whistleblower." Some journalists, largely in Europe, have begun writing with the English word "whistleblower," for lack of a better local term. This might prove beneficial over time, as the connotation of the word is largely understood to be positive to the public.[13][14]

Whatever context you are in, consider the words that will be used to describe you and consider the perceptions that people might bring to their judgement of you. Be prepared, and consider your tactics accordingly. Rather than let your adversaries control the narrative, it's better to get out ahead of the story. Consider carefully the words you use to portray yourself, your actions, and the actions of those around you. These are often the words that others will use, too.

Contexts

The environment you find yourself in can make it easier or harder to disclose information. This could be the culture of the company you work for, the local or regional government, or even more broadly, the cultural norms of your region or country. Let's consider a range of contexts that you might find yourself in and think through the perceptions and obstacles that are unique to each one.

Around the World

Those who stand up to power by exposing the truth are needed wherever corruption is high. That can be pretty much anywhere. After all, most countries around the world have high levels of corruption. Transparency International, the global coalition against corruption, annually authors a Corruption Perceptions Index that tracks levels of corruption throughout the world. In this case, corruption is defined as "the abuse of entrusted power for private gain," which could be within government, in the private sector, or on a local level, such as being forced to pay a bribe at a traffic stop. In the 2018 report, the numbers showed little to no change in countries with moderate to high levels of corruption. As the authors noted, "more than two-thirds of countries score below 50, while the average score is just 43. Perhaps most disturbing is that the vast majority of countries assessed have made little to no progress. Only twenty have made significant progress in recent years." If corruption is nearly ubiquitous around the world, then there is ample opportunity—and much need—to expose it.

Unfortunately, the places where corruption is highest are often the places where it's difficult to challenge power. If a normal part of business involves taking money under the table or paying off the police, exposing these practices will be difficult. This isn't just because the allegations might fall on deaf ears. Rather, it's because the system is set against you before you even begin. In places like this, you will likely have individuals and organizations actively trying to stop you. You will be up against a culture of corruption, not just an individual or a single act.

From Papua New Guinea, which ranked 138 out of 180 countries for corruption in 2018, comes an emblematic example of success in challenging rotten government. Simon Eyork, the chairperson of a school in a village there, had been promised funds by the government to make structural improvements to his school and other schools. For more than two years, Eyork went to authorities asking when the funds would be dispersed. He was repeatedly pushed off and told to come back later. Finally, officials asked for a hefty payoff of 30,000 kina ($13,000 USD) to process his payments.

Instead of paying or going to the police directly, Eyork did his own research and approached Transparency International's Advocacy and Legal Advice Centre in Papua New Guinea. Together they went to the police, conducted a sting operation, and then presented their case to the media. This in turn caused other schools to come forward who were also missing payments. With pressure from the media and public, the authorities soon capitulated and funded the schools. Eyork's school received its funding and he was able to use it for infrastructure improvements. By seeking out a partner instead of going directly to the police—who likely would have done nothing—Eyork was able to work with the center to develop a sophisticated plan to pressure the government to do the right thing.[15] In many countries where corruption levels are high, working with the media to exert public pressure is the only way to win.

Fighting Bribery

Crowdsourced recording of bribery has become an active element in fighting corruption. In 2010, I Paid a Bribe (https://www.ipaidabribe.com) was launched in India and is currently available in 15 countries, with 14 more pending at the time of this writing. The site allows users to record when they've been made to pay a bribe: for example, when applying for a passport, when stopped by a traffic cop, or when trying to get electricity turned on at home. In the last eight years, the site has received over 175,000 reports, totaling more than $400 million lost to corruption.[16] Tracking bribes is a great first step to reducing bribery by taking the issue out of the darkness, allowing those in power to see the corruption and giving them the opportunity to do something about it. I Paid a Bribe is a simple way to disclose information by reporting corrupt practices online. Of course, people reporting must be careful to only leave a minimum of information, so they can avoid retaliation. Think about your specific context and give any info a gut check before submitting it.

When dealing with a broader issue of corruption that spans multiple countries, it may be advantageous to point out the corruption in a country with a better record and reputation.

Perhaps this could have been a factor in the choice of John Doe, who released records of the Panamanian law firm Mossack Fonseca. He chose to work with a German newspaper instead of a Panamanian one. In the Corruption Perceptions Index, Germany ranked 11th out of 180 countries in 2018, making it one of the least corrupt countries, while Panama ranked 93rd. This level of corruption in Panama, along with the corresponding cultural context, might have led to the disclosures being stifled and made it harder to speak up safely. The environment you find yourself in can potentially be a huge deterrent to reporting corruption and other wrongdoing.

Alongside the perceived level of existing corruption in a location, specific historical and social contexts in countries and communities can make it easier or harder to disclose information. In Germany, for example, the history of secret police in East Germany has left a negative association attached to being an informer. Germany has had two separate secret police systems that have utilized citizen informers: first was the Gestapo under Adolf Hitler, then came the Ministry for State Security (Stasi) under the German Democratic Republic. By 1989, the Stasi employed 97,000 individuals, but had an additional 174,000 people contributing to their network of informers in a population of 17 million. As professor Judith Rauhofer writes, this created a ratio of one observer for every sixty-three citizens. It has only been 30 years since 1989, and being an informer in this culture is still largely viewed as a bad thing. It's fortunate that Germany's perceived levels of corruption are low, as the historical context could make it difficult to disclose information about corruption.[17][18]

Historical contexts can also take the form of standards in a culture that have developed over time. For example, Japan has a strong cultural hierarchy in business. This societal context could have been a factor in the recent Olympus scandal.

Michael Woodford, a longtime employee, was appointed CEO of Olympus in 2011. He was the first non-Japanese person to hold the position at the camera company. Soon after accepting the position, Woodford exposed, through the help of an anonymous employee, the payment of over $500 million to a series of companies in the United States and places like the Cayman Islands.[19] [20] The transfers could not be explained at the time, though they were later determined to be payments to hide years of company losses.[21] An independent report conducted in December 2011 stated that "an atmosphere was cultivated in which objections were not allowed to be spoken" and that "there were many yes men among the directors [...] the Board of Directors had become a mere formality."[22] This type of cultural hierarchy stifling the exposure of truth isn't unique to Olympus or Japan: it can be found around the world.

Corporate Culture

A workplace can put many pressures on an individual to keep them from speaking up. A job is your livelihood and you might be supporting a family. For most employees, losing a job is a disaster. It can be incredibly hard to speak up when so much is on the line. Even more so, most corporate contexts don't support those who stand up. Instead, roadblocks are put up and people who try to expose the truth often face retaliation.

Some companies have gotten the message: they need to cultivate cultures where speaking up is encouraged and supported. Evidence has shown that employees who speak up about wrongdoing can be a canary in the coal mine, catching a larger issue early on, ultimately saving money, jobs, and sometimes the company itself.[23]

Tom Devine's book *The Corporate Whistleblower's Survival Guide* shows how important those who report wrongdoing are for companies. Devine outlines the value of policies that support and reward those who expose wrongdoing. Such policies create an environment where individuals feel safe in speaking up. Safe disclosure policies can prevent issues from spinning out of control into settlements or litigation. In fact, Devine notes, "some insurance companies are offering corporate clients who go this route 1 to 2 percent off their general liability premiums."[24] [25]

If insurance companies see liabilities reduced by corporations that encourage employees to speak out, it follows that such transparency is generally good for business. Sadly, no matter what the insurance providers say, retaliation against employees remains rampant in many corporate cultures.

Linda Almonte filed as a whistleblower with the SEC in 2010 under the Dodd-Frank Act to report $250 million in fraud by JPMorgan Chase.[26] [27] She initially reported the fraud internally, but rather than being applauded by her bosses, she was fired. Reporting the fraud was "essentially suicide," Almonte told HuffPost.[28] Additional retaliation from the bank included heavy surveillance of herself and her family.

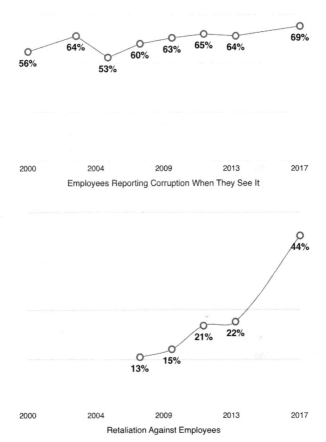

56%
64%
53%
60%
63%
65%
64%
69%

2000   2004   2009   2013   2017

Employees Reporting Corruption When They See It

44%

13%
15%
21%
22%

2000   2004   2009   2013   2017

Retaliation Against Employees

Data from the 2018 Global Business Ethics Survey.

The Global Business Ethics Survey in 2018 found that 69 percent of corporate employees reported corruption when they observed it, up from 53 percent in 2005.[29] In other words, people are speaking up more. This is good! Unfortunately, the same survey found that 44 percent of the time employees are retaliated against for exposing wrongs. This is up from 22 percent in 2013, a doubling of the rate of retaliation in only four years. Although people are speaking up more, they are also being retaliated against more often.

In 2018, a source inside Elon Musk's Gigafactory in Nevada tipped off *Business Insider* about raw materials that needed to be reworked or thrown out in the factory. The source, Martin Tripp, provided documents that suggested that this may have cost the company at least $150 million. *Business Insider* did not name Tripp, but the leak so enraged Musk that he made it a personal mission to identify Tripp and destroy him. As reported in a Bloomberg story, not only did the company sue Tripp for $167 million, the security department at Tesla also gave a tip to the local sheriff's department alleging that Tripp was planning a mass shooting at the Gigafactory, an unusual but effective form of retaliation.[30] [31] [32]

If you find yourself in a corporate culture where it's clear that those who speak up aren't supported, take your time and weigh your options. There are many other ways to expose wrongdoing safely.

Sexual Harassment

Whether it occurs in the corporate context or elsewhere, sexual harassment is highly underreported. An analysis of a decade of sexual harassment research found that victims only go to a supervisor, manager, or union representative to report a sexual harassment incident in the workplace one-quarter to one-third of the time. Formal reports are filed in only a fraction of those cases, keeping sexual harassment largely unseen.[33] Many factors further stifle speaking up. A 2016 *Harvard Business Review* report cites a few other factors: masculine cultures, the bystander effect, and most notably, the fear of retaliation.[34] [35]

In many workplaces, masculine cultures can permit sexual harassment or even a boys' club environment. Positions of power are largely held by men, and individuals tend to demonstrate their power over others to secure their status among the group. Women in these environments are frequently less likely to speak up because they fear that nothing will change—or that if it does change, it will only change for the worse, leading to retaliation. Additionally, there may be no human resources department to take complaints (this has been a problem in technology startup cultures). Or there may be an incentive to downplay sexual harassment in order to get along at the company and be promoted.[36] [37] [38]

The bystander effect can also discourage reporting sexual harassment. When multiple bystanders witness violations, they're often less likely to speak up about it or intervene. This makes the entire group or organization less likely to recognize or report such violations. Inaction on the part of others has the effect of implicitly condoning the act. Even if no one explicitly laughs the harassment off or condones the harassment, having multiple bystanders remain inactive makes it far less likely that the victim will report it.

The fear of retaliation is likely the most significant reason that harassment goes unreported. Those who are harassed are often afraid of losing their jobs, of losing their reputation in their industry, of being unable to get another job, of being labeled as troublemakers, of being bad-mouthed in the media, or even of being blamed for inciting the harassment.[39] [40] [41]

In the midst of the #MeToo movement, Roger Ailes and subsequently Bill O'Reilly were exposed as serial harassers in the Fox News workplace. Yet in response to the mounting evidence that the masculine culture was one component to blame, 21st Century Fox defended itself, saying that "no current or former Fox News employee ever took advantage of the 21st Century Fox hotline to raise a concern about Bill O'Reilly, even anonymously."[42] This highlights that even contemporary reporting tools put in place by companies, such as anonymous hotlines, may not actually be safe (as we will see later on). Sometimes it's not the method of reporting that needs to change in order to fix underreporting. Instead, the culture and environment must change.[43]

The #MeToo movement has shone light on many of these issues, but unfortunately many people in the world still do not have the same legal protections offered in countries like the United States. In the United States, sexual harassment is a prohibited form of sex discrimination, violating Title VII of the Civil Rights Act of 1964.[44] A 2017 report by WORLD Policy Analysis Center at the University of California, Los Angeles, noted that more than a third of all countries do not have these types of protections in place. This shortcoming has limited safe employment opportunities for many women in the world, preventing them from becoming economically autonomous.[45]

U.S. Government

Public sector employees in particular have found themselves vilified for speaking up publicly. Though many governments have passed laws that protect disclosure, those who choose to stand up and expose wrongdoing within governments are still bullied, retaliated against, and stigmatized.

David Pozen, a law professor at Columbia University, has argued that governments actually need unsanctioned disclosures to serve as a "safety valve." While governments may externally attack and vilify those who disclose information to the public, those same governments are willing to condone anonymous leaks that serve an administration's goals. Controlled leaks by the government allow those in power a "highly salient mode of disclosure," Pozen wrote in his 2013 *Harvard Law Review* article, "The Leaky Leviathan: Why the Government Condemns and Condones Unlawful Disclosures of Information."

Pozen wrote that a strategic leak's "promise of authentic revelation, its association with palace intrigue, its whiff of illegality—all help to whet reader appetites and generate front-page coverage." He argued that leaks open a way to speak to the public without appearing to condone the act of leaking information. Unfortunately, for individuals ready to expose wrongs within the government, this creates a double standard: leaks that serve those in power are tolerated or even encouraged, and leaks that challenge power are not. [46]

The United States is a perfect example of this dichotomy. America has strong free speech and whistleblower protection laws compared to many governments around the world. Yet recent administrations have attacked leaking with a vengeance. This shift ramped up under President Obama through new "insider threat" programs and the prosecution of whistleblowers. These trends have continued under President Trump, exacerbated by not only more prosecutions, but also by Trump's public criticism of leakers.[47] Put together, these actions create a chilling effect on speaking up. To some Americans, leaking has become akin to treason.

When Obama took office in 2009, he promised to create an "unprecedented level of openness in government," explaining that "openness will strengthen our democracy."[48] He even went so far as to make public commitments to transparency and accountability, especially for whistleblowers. On Change.gov, this was laid out with a statement that the administration would "empower federal employees as watchdogs of wrongdoing and partners in performance." The statement went on to promise that Obama's ethics agenda would "ensure that federal agencies expedite the process for reviewing whistleblower claims" and that whistleblowers would "have full access to courts and due process."[49]

Despite the administration's stated goal of transparency, it became clear as Obama moved into his second term in office that it would be a restrictive administration. Rather than openness and transparency, the real goal was to direct exactly what and how information was released to the public. Through social media and the White House website, bits of information were released to keep up the appearance of openness. Yet rarely was there enough for journalists to conduct real investigations, as Leonard Downie Jr., former executive editor of the *Washington Post* has argued. He has said that the Obama administration's war on leaks and other efforts to control information were the most aggressive that he'd seen since the Nixon administration.[50, 51]

This war on those who try to expose wrongs to the public was made no more apparent than by Obama's initiation of an insider threat program throughout the federal government. On October

7, 2011, Obama declared Presidential Order 13587, "Structural Reforms to Improve the Security of Classified Networks and the Responsible Sharing and Safeguarding of Classified Information." This order came in the wake of the Chelsea Manning and WikiLeaks releases. The order, among other requirements, called for the creation of an Insider Threat Task Force that would develop and oversee a "government-wide policy for the deterrence, detection, and mitigation of insider threats."[52]

In general, these insider threat programs encourage employees to be on the lookout for coworkers who might harm the organization by releasing unapproved information. In the corporate setting this might mean identifying employees who might be selling or who might be open to selling trade secrets to other companies. Within the government this largely focuses on determining who might be a spy—who might be selling or releasing classified information. Beyond just keeping an eye out, coworkers are encouraged to report on each other for suspicious behavior.

The presidential order required the implementation of insider threat reporting programs in all federal agencies. Such programs create the potential for a Stasi-era atmosphere, where neighbors police neighbors. The training materials for the insider threat program instructed government workers to look out for coworkers who exhibit "questionable national loyalty," which might include "displaying questionable loyalty to U.S. government or company" or "making anti-U.S. comments."[53] Jesselyn Radack, who heads the Whistleblower and Source Protection Program (WHISPeR) at ExposeFacts, decried this as a return to McCarthyism.[54]

every leak makes us weak

CDSE Center for Development of Security Excellence

This poster was produced to advertise "Insider Threat Programs" within the U.S. government. The poster was eventually removed and replaced by a whistle-blower-supportive poster after complaints were filed by the Project on Government Oversight.

This insider threat program has stifled those who want to use their free speech rights to speak out. It's important to remember that in the United States, you can legally speak freely to the press or others about things your organization is doing as long as that information isn't protected under a legal contract. Even "legal" contracts such as nondisclosure clauses have been found to be illegal because they restrict individuals' rights to free speech.

Leaks Are Not Illegal

In the United States you have the right to free speech—
you can legally share (even with the media) information
that isn't restricted or classified. Such was the case with
James Comey's "leak" of his contemporaneous notes
after meeting with Donald Trump. Because his notes
didn't contain secret or classified material, it wasn't illegal
to release them publicly. Even the fact that Comey chose
to do so through an intermediary does not make the act
illegal.[55] This right to free speech includes your personal
opinions about situations at work, as long as your comments don't violate an agreement that you've signed. Of
course, in many situations your employer also has the
right to fire you, so assess your circumstances carefully.

The Obama administration had one other powerful way of stifling
disclosure to the public and limiting the free speech of government
employees. This was through the prosecution of leakers. When
Obama took office in 2009, there had been only one previous prosecution for providing material to the press under the Espionage
Act of 1917.[56] During his time in office, Obama's administration
brought cases against eight people on charges of violating this act. [57]

The Espionage Act is a draconian law originally created to
prosecute spies and traitors in the nationwide anti-foreigner hys-
teria leading up to World War I. In the 100-plus years since it was
enacted, the use of the Espionage Act has drastically evolved. As
currently interpreted, the law equates providing information to the
press with treason. This tars those who leak classified information

to the press with the same brush as those who try to help foreign actors undermine U.S. national security. [58]

Daniel Ellsberg, who was also charged under the Espionage Act (the charges were later dropped), has argued that the act needs reform. As it is currently being interpreted, the mere act of giving classified information to the press is illegal—even if the information shows that the government or someone within the government has done something illegal. As Edward Snowden said, "I would love to go back and face a fair trial, but unfortunately . . . there is no fair trial available, on offer right now." [59] It would be impossible for him to receive a fair trial under the Espionage Act because his defense would not be able to argue that the information he released pertained to illegal activities, which would then give him justification for the release. [60] [61] With the Espionage Act in place, those who see illegal activity within the government have limited ways to disclose this information for the good of the public. The Espionage Act creates a strong deterrent because speaking up can make you an enemy of the state. As a result, federal employees are far less likely to talk to the press for fear that they will be prosecuted. [62]

In fact, those who speak to or work with the press in the United States are sometimes treated far more harshly than elsewhere in the world. Reality Winner, who was found guilty of leaking a single document to *The Intercept* in 2017, was given a sentence comparable to that of Paul Manafort, a former campaign manager for Donald Trump who was convicted of tax fraud, bank fraud, and the failure to disclose a foreign bank account. [63]

When Winner first went before a judge, she was cited as a flight risk and denied bail. The twenty-five year old had been accused of leaking a U.S. intelligence document showing that the Russian government had actively tried to hack the U.S. presidential election. Though Winner had no history of unethical or illegal behavior and had an excellent record as an Air Force linguist for six years, she was denied bail.[64] This left Winner in a small-town jail for a year while her trial progressed.[65]

By comparison, Paul Manafort was allowed to post bail and live comfortably in his home with an ankle-monitoring device. Even more bizarre was the fact that a judge allowed him to travel to one of his other homes in the Hamptons to host a party for Christmas. The argument was that his $2.7 million home in Virginia was not adequate to host the party.[66] The United States clearly has a two-tiered justice system where the rich are able to pay to make their lives easier. The message is clear—unless you are already rich and powerful, if you talk to the press, the government will come after you.

Overall, the treatment and sentences of those who disclose information to the press are out of proportion to other crimes. These sentences only serve to create an atmosphere of anxiety for public employees, leaving them with limited options with respect to speaking up about illegal activities that they see internally and that might drastically affect the public.

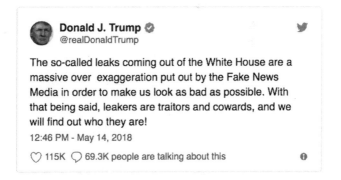

Donald J. Trump ✓
@realDonaldTrump

The so-called leaks coming out of the White House are a massive over exaggeration put out by the Fake News Media in order to make us look as bad as possible. With that being said, leakers are traitors and cowards, and we will find out who they are!

12:46 PM - May 14, 2018

♡ 115K ⚲ 69.3K people are talking about this

The tactics put in place under the Obama administration have been exacerbated by the Trump administration. Under Trump, the government has presented even more criticism and obstacles for those who choose to use their free speech rights to talk to the press. On August 4, 2017, Attorney General Jeff Sessions and Director of National Intelligence Dan Coats (who together co-chair the Insider Threat Task Force) gave a press conference outlining their plans to stop federal leakers altogether. "For those out there who may be listening or watching these announcements," said Coats, "if you improperly disclose classified information, we will find you. We will investigate you. We will prosecute you to the fullest extent of the law, and you will not be happy with the result."

The attacks on those who speak to the press have gone further under Trump by actually attacking the free press itself. Through a new indictment of Julian Assange, the U.S. Department of Justice will be charging Assange and WikiLeaks for publishing classified material.[67] The indictment raises new questions of freedom of the press under the First Amendment, and questions about WikiLeaks' role as a publisher. Under the Obama administration, the Justice Department had backed off an Assange prosecution because of the historical and legal protections for publishers under the Constitution.[68] These renewed attacks are likely driven by Trump's public decrying of the entire media, legitimate or otherwise.

Legal Protections

Before we dive into the varied legal contexts for those who disclose information, let's just say this: before you do anything, talk to a lawyer. Each situation is unique, and determining when certain laws apply or don't apply is too difficult for the average citizen to sift through. A lawyer can help you understand not only the legal contexts, but also the pros and cons of each method of disclosing. Furthermore, consulting a lawyer adds a layer of much-needed caution if you are in a country where activists are targeted, where free speech is squashed, and where your ability to speak out is controlled or stifled by the government. Even if there are laws in place to protect disclosure, be sure to listen to your instincts, and seek legal counsel if you're concerned.

Around the world, legal protections for those who disclose information are widely varied. Laws vary by country, by the type of industry, and by the type of information being released. As you assess your own context, consider any whistleblower-specific laws. While the actual legal protections may not apply to your situation, disclosing in a country with whistleblower laws in place means that the culture has already evolved to support and protect those who disclose.

Some countries, such as Hungary, have established one overarching law, while other countries, such as the United States, have a rat's nest of more than sixty laws that depend on specific circumstances. But most countries, such as Denmark, Finland, Spain, and the majority of countries in Africa, have no laws whatsoever to protect whistleblowers.[69] [70] In 2013, before Brexit, only four of the twenty-seven EU member countries had comprehensive legal frameworks protecting whistleblowing on the part of both private- and public-sector employees. These four countries were Luxembourg, Romania, Slovenia, and the U.K. Of the remaining countries, sixteen had partial protections and seven had none at all.[71] [72] On a positive note, in early 2019 a new European Union agreement was set up to create a legally binding whistleblower directive to establish consistent, minimum standards for all member nations.[73] [74]

The United Nations could adopt a broad mandate to support whistleblowers and freedom of expression. Unfortunately, the UN didn't issue its own Whistleblower Protection Policy for disclosures about practices within the UN itself until 2005,[75] and some have noted that implementation of the law has been rendered ineffective in practice.[76]

One systemic issue for the legal protection of those who disclose is that laws typically provide only partial coverage. Protections are inconsistent and the most common prohibition is against retaliation. Even in the United States, where the legal protections for whistleblowers and those who disclose are relatively strong, no single law defines these protections. Instead, an inconsistent, messy mix of federal and state laws describe particular circumstances under which disclosure is protected.

For example, the Whistleblower Protection Act (WPA), enacted in 1989, covers federal employees who choose to report corruption, but it doesn't cover state or private employees.[77] Its statutory boundaries have also been shrinking thanks to new loopholes and prerequisites. Congress restored the original WPA rights in the Whistleblower Protection Enhancement Act (WPEA) in 2012.[78] That same year, Congress finally created government-wide coverage for federal contractor whistleblowers in laws with separate enforcement structures from those for civil servants.[79] This type of piecemeal legislation is rampant in countries that have laws to protect disclosure. Once again, you should consult a lawyer before you get in too deep.

The type of information that you release plays a factor in whether existing laws protect the disclosure. If you have signed employee contracts or nondisclosure agreements, or if you have agreed to certain stipulations as part of a settlement agreement, you may not be able to say certain things publicly or release certain pieces of information. In the United States, there is currently a backlash against forced arbitration clauses that limit the legal rights of workers who might otherwise sue for discrimination or sue for wrongful termination when they are treated unjustly in the workplace.[80] Be sure to consider what you have signed, and your legal obligations under those agreements, before you disclose. A contemporary example of this is the case of Stormy Daniels, who was paid $130,000 by President Donald Trump prior to the 2016 election in exchange for signing a nondisclosure agreement about their alleged affair.[81] Fortunately all federal whistleblower laws implemented since 2000 have had "anti-gag" provisions, preventing nondisclosure agreements from trumping free-speech rights.[82]

Similar factors come into play with respect to the type of information you are preparing to release. Corporations have used "company property" and "trade secrets" as reasons to fight against disclosure, either claiming (a) theft on the grounds that the information wasn't the employee's to take and release, or (b) that the information was a proprietary secret of the company. In 2016, Congress passed the Defend Trade Secrets Act to protect trade secrets, while at the same time carving out specific protections for whistleblowers who seek to expose corrupt practices that involve trade secrets.[83] Though these goals are certainly laudable, the interpretation by the courts, particularly in the case of Timothy Loftus, has had the opposite effect on whistleblower protection.

In 2016, Loftus took home a few boxes of information from his job at insurance company Unum Group and provided them to his lawyer to assess his possible whistleblower rights.[84] As the original law was intended, Loftus should have been immunized against being sued by Unum Group for taking company property or trade secrets. Unfortunately, the courts decided otherwise and allowed Unum to go after Loftus. As Peter S. Menell, co-director of the Berkeley Center for Law & Technology, wrote: "The court's order also undermines the very investigatory and reporting activities specifically authorized by the DTSA, the False Claims Act, the Dodd-Frank Act, and various other whistleblower statutes and protections." [85]

In addition to laws protecting trade secrets, certain industries have lobbied to put in place unique laws to constrain what can and cannot be disclosed. The agricultural industry in the United States has worked to establish a number of state-level laws (known as "ag-gag" laws) that make it illegal to film or document conditions on a farm without approval of the owner.[86] Essentially, this is anti-whistleblower legislation, criminalizing video or other exposures of cruelty to animals and other unethical acts in commercial agriculture. If you are contemplating disclosure, you must do more research—or make sure your lawyer does it—to understand whether you might be affected by unique laws.

Government intelligence employees, particularly in the U.S., have had an extremely difficult time disclosing the truth. By definition, it is illegal to share classified information with anyone who does not have the proper and appropriate clearance level to view the information. That is a huge roadblock for disclosing information about unethical, illegal, or otherwise corrupt actions tucked away in classified material. The act of disclosure itself will be regarded as illegal. This is the basis for almost all of the notable government whistleblower cases, including those of Daniel Ellsberg, Thomas Drake, John Kiriakou, Chelsea Manning, Edward Snowden, Jeffrey Sterling, and Reality Winner. In all of these cases, the Espionage Act of 1917 was used to bring charges.

To protect themselves, governments are classifying more and more information. Something that wasn't even classified a few years ago might be top secret today. This is particularly evident in the United States, where even a report by U.S. intelligence agencies on their own overclassification wasn't released to the public, as HuffPost reported in 2014.[87]

No matter the context you find yourself in, things will be legally tricky if you end up in court. Talk to a lawyer and use the best practices in the rest of this book to make sure that you are as safe as possible when disclosing information.

Your Data Will Be Used Against You

You are your data.

That might sound like a broad statement, unless you consider how much data you produce with digital devices every day or even every minute. Who can gain access to that data? Anybody who wants to know about you and who has the power to tap into all that information. As someone attempting to disclose information, you will have many adversaries. Some will try to stop you. Some will be poised to retaliate against you. You need to understand the data trails that you leave behind, how the data is collected, and who has access to it. Only then can you be more strategic with respect to your digital habits and disclosure techniques.

In this section we will consider who might tap into your data and how. The point of this exercise isn't to make you stop using technology. On the contrary, it is to help you develop enough of an understanding that you can make smart choices about how and when you use digital technology. You must protect yourself, and to do that you must protect your data.

I could write a whole book exploring the landscape of the digital data that you produce, along with the many surveillance techniques used to collect this data. Fortunately, many others have already worked on this topic. Bruce Schneier's book *Data and Goliath* is particularly useful for thinking through these issues and offers a number of possible solutions. If you want to dig deeper on data, that book is a great resource. However, the easiest and most logical place to start thinking about data trails and tracking is likely within your arm's reach right now: your smartphone.

These marvelous devices have reshaped our relationship with information. They're ubiquitous computers that fit in our pockets, are always with us, and are always connected. They maximize connectivity with a minimum of effort. We have our friends, families, jobs, and the information of the world at our fingertips. But, of course, with constant connection comes constant tracking.

These devices hold more personal information than a filing cabinet ever could. Yet most people are quite relaxed with their smartphones' security, either because they choose not to care or they don't know how to secure them. Think about it. We are armed with powerful digital devices in our pockets. They have relaxed security features that leak data constantly. And plenty of corporations, governments, and even individuals are happy to sit on the other end of the internet, hoovering up our data. When they are our adversaries, they can use this data against us.

The device manufacturers (e.g., Apple), application providers (e.g., Facebook), and internet service providers (e.g., AT&T) gather your data from these devices and monetize it. A smartphone has so many sources of information that it's hard to list them all. But consider that a phone has microphones, cameras, and location chips and is used for many modes of communication—email, text, phone calls, and more. If gathered and put together, the data moving in and out of our smartphones reveals a detailed, frighteningly detailed picture of who we are and probably even what we think. Regardless of whether you believe that the value proposition of trading data access for free software is fair or ethical, it is the world we live in today. Your data is being vacuumed up, stored, and sold.

You should be wary of your smartphone and the ways that it can be tracked. One example of smartphone data tracking comes from Malte Spitz, a member of the German Green Party. He requested and received six months of his location metadata that was collected and stored at T-Mobile. This data wasn't being collected by some illegal spyware, but rather was gathered under the EU Data Retention Directive that was in place from 2006 until 2014. That directive required telecommunications companies to save the IP address and time stamp of every email, text message, or phone call sent or received by a user. Malte's six months of information included 35,830 individual data points. When mapped, these data points produced a finely detailed view of his life.[88]

Perhaps an even more important treasure trove of information is the actual audio and video that can be captured by your phone, potentially without your knowledge. Phones have been hacked, either by installing software on them directly or by convincing individuals to click on links that compromise their devices. By compromising your device, then listening directly to conversations or remotely watching videos taken surreptitiously from your phone, a nefarious third party can potentially learn almost everything about you—except perhaps the thoughts you hold secret in your head. Actually, sometimes what we do on the internet unwittingly reveals our innermost thoughts, fears, and desires. As early as 2006, the FBI was remotely turning on cell phone microphones to eavesdrop on conversations.[89] In recent years, software available online can be installed on someone else's phone, allowing remote listening, viewing, and tracking.[90] [91]

Sometimes the data recorded is used for more banal purposes than direct monetization. Consider the log files of your IP address, which offer a record of when you connect to a company server. This information would seem to be valueless data for a company, except to be able to debug a problem with your software. But this type of boring metadata can still have consequences for an individual: an IP address can be geolocated, and if the data is time-stamped, it can reveal the user's physical location at a certain time. When a corporation or someone else who can look at this type of data is your adversary, they can track your movements.

Let's say you're browsing the web on a laptop. You might think that as long as you don't log in to any services, and as long as you use a web browser in incognito mode or with private browsing enabled, it will be difficult to track your identity on the web. On the contrary, enough variables are transmitted to a server by your web browser alone to make your laptop unique and in effect fingerprintable. When you visit a webpage, your browser shares such variables as the fonts you have installed, your screen size, the dimensions of your browser window, any plugins you have installed, the exact browser version you have installed, and much more. The variables transmitted to the server make every computer browser close to mathematically unique. You can even be tracked as you browse the web, regardless of whether you use a VPN (Virtual Private Network) to mask your IP address.[92] Go see how unique your browser is and what you can do about it with the Electronic Frontier Foundation's Panopticlick website (https://panopticlick.eff.org).

No matter the type of disclosure you are attempting or the context you find yourself in, if you use digital technology (i.e., if you're basically anyone besides Vladimir Putin), you should con-sider digital technology corporations as your adversaries.[93] Cor-porations—not nonprofits, and generally not governments—are the controllers of the devices and services that we rely on. Think of the applications on your phone. Almost all of them were likely created by various companies. Our reliance on these organiza-tions means that we are interacting with them constantly, thereby giving them data about us. If you are going to try to disclose information safely, you need to understand not only your own process of disclosure, but also how third parties might track you or otherwise gather data about you.

Let's start by imagining that you work at one of the large cor-porations whose services you use, e.g., Google. If you had the authority to look at your own data, what could you see? Among other things, you might see your personal messages to friends and family, photos of where you've been with your friends' faces identi-fied, the websites you've visited, your purchase history, and perhaps even the temperature in your home.[94] If this data is put together, it would paint quite a picture of your habits, including when you're home, whether you're having an affair, or the fact that you might be pregnant.[95] [96] With smartphones, this data is collected regardless of whether you are actually at your computer working or simply surfing the web.

A number of projects have tried to make people aware of the oversharing of location data on the internet. In 2010, Please Rob Me got quite a lot of attention for analyzing a user's Twitter handle to see what location data they had shared about their home and whether they were at home at the time of a post.[97] I Know Where Your Cat Lives made a similar statement about our oversharing habits by using cats as surrogates for humans. An interactive map of the world allows you to explore pictures of cats taken around the world with geolocated data. Browsing your neighborhood, you can quickly see a cat you recognize and where it lives.[98]

In 2015, a team of researchers discovered that a Samsung smart fridge was vulnerable to attack and might give out a user's Google log-in information.[99] Devices such as cars, thermostats, refrigerators, security systems, health trackers, watches, and the general "digital personal assistants" that make up the Internet of Things are becoming "smart" by being connected to the internet constantly, all under the auspices of optimizing our lives. These all add more data points that can be used to make accurate inferences about your behaviors and thoughts.

Stalk Yourself

As an exercise, try searching for yourself on the internet. Adopt the mindset of one of your adversaries and create a dossier on yourself. Even better, hire a firm to do it. This way, when you face an adversary, you will already know what's out there, and you will be ready to react when someone tries to use the information against you. You can also work on removing or hiding information that might be publicly available about you, making it harder to find.

If this data were secured behind lock and key on company servers or deleted shortly after it was created, it wouldn't be a big deal. Unfortunately, companies are monetizing our data, and selling it to data brokers and others. A 2019 Motherboard article reported that for only $300, you can gain access to someone's location history and even live-track their phone.[100] All you need is the right contact in the bail industry. Your data is out there, and it is cheaply available. If a reporter can get your information for $300, consider what a powerful adversary such as a company, government, or law enforcement agency can get.

In 2013, Edward Snowden drew back the veil on the contemporary surveillance state in the United States, England, and other European countries. He revealed a state of mass surveillance on a scale almost no one outside of the intelligence community could have fathomed. As of 2013, the U.S. National Security Agency was bulk-collecting internet traffic, sifting through it, and storing metadata associated with millions of web users. The NSA collected Americans' phone records and revealed intricate networks of personal connections across the globe. The agency had secret agreements with the largest digital companies. After approval from a secret court, it could requisition, on demand, a user's emails and other content stored in the cloud. Bulk collection feels very Orwellian, and questions of its legality have bounced back and forth in the courts.[101] [102] [103]

We might want to believe that in the years since the Snowden revelations, intelligence agencies have reduced their collection of information. But of course, information is power, and until the people force their governments to stop, they won't stop. Instead, we are seeing governments gather more power, not less. In early 2018, the U.S. House of Representatives voted to extend the warrantless surveillance law that the NSA uses to gather and sift through electronic communications and phone calls of Americans, so that foreigners communicating with Americans could be targeted more easily.[104]

In 2016, the Russian government put in place laws that require internet and telecom companies to save all communication records and metadata for at least six months, as well as to provide back doors to encryption so that the government can read any information. These measures, of course, were ushered in under the rhetoric of anti-terrorism.[105]

One last point about phones: corporations and governments have been pouring fantastic amounts of money into voice recognition technology, basically to accomplish two technical feats. The first and most familiar is "speech to text." This enables the computer's digital assistants—such as Alexa on Amazon devices, Google Assistant, or Siri on Apple devices—to understand what we say, to answer our questions, and to follow our commands. It also allows eavesdropping on our calls. Your conversation can therefore be automatically transcribed into text and made searchable. By 2005, the NSA had the capability of "Google for Voice," allowing content from phone calls to be transcribed in this fashion.[106] The other technical focus has been on voice-printing. This is essentially a unique thumbprint for your voice, allowing your supposedly anonymous conversations to be tied back to your identity.[107] It is similar to facial recognition technology, which identifies you by your physical appearance. But the voice itself is actually much harder to disguise than one's face. Human Rights Watch reports that the Chinese government is working on a national voice biometric database, with the goal of making all of its citizens uniquely identifiable by voice.[108]

In another example of mass tracking from China, cities are rolling out CCTV cameras equipped with facial recognition technology. Some Chinese cities already have enough cameras to track everyone who lives, works, or visits. The BBC reported in late 2017 that China had 170 million CCTV cameras installed across the country, with an additional 400 million slated to be installed and operational by the end of 2020. In a video piece by the BBC, it took the local authorities only seven minutes to identify and apprehend a British journalist as he walked around a city in China.[109]

In the United States and across the world, law enforcement has been using Stingrays, also known as cell-site simulators or IMSI catchers. These devices simulate cell phone towers and can analyze and record the cell phone data that goes through them. Imagine if you wanted to monitor someone's cell phone activity. Instead of going to court to subpoena T-Mobile for the customer's data, you could simply set up a Stingray device outside their house and allow their phone to connect to it. You could then just sit there monitoring and recording their activity. Amazingly, these devices aren't illegal in the United States, and most agencies refuse to tell the public whether they are using them. Most states do not require a warrant prior to the use of these devices. The ACLU has done a nice job of compiling press reports and publicly accessible documents on the use of these devices across the United States. As of November 2018, seventy-five agencies owned Stingrays, but the ACLU noted that this figure may be low, because many agencies don't disclose the purchase or use of these devices to the public.[110]

The ACLU has also been exposing the use of license plate data in the United States. In particular, it has called out U.S. Immigration and Customs Enforcement over its use of license plate data from more than 80 law enforcement organizations.[111] ICE has been analyzing huge data sets that were collected by automated license plate readers from multiple states. These devices are either cameras in public spaces that track and record license plates, or vehicles with many cameras mounted to them that drive around scanning license plates from cars. ICE is trying to identify undocumented immigrants with this data, but imagine if your adversary had this technology. You would have to ditch your car for a bike or public transport, or find other ways of getting around. Predictive policing like this is still in its infancy, and like the use of Stingrays, it's being implemented in stealth, out of the public eye.[112] [113]

Suppose you work in law enforcement and, like Frank Serpico, you're ready to blow the whistle on corruption on the inside. Or maybe you work at a large digital company and are ready to expose unethical policies to the public. Perhaps you are simply trying to escape an unsafe working situation and warn other potential victims. Whatever the case, you must realize that you are currently emitting enough information with your phone and other devices that you can easily be located and monitored, even for the low price of $300. Furthermore, others are actively monitoring populations of which you may be a part, gathering data, keeping it, and analyzing it. If your adversary has the capabilities to access this information, you will be quickly marked.

Frankly, we're still just at the beginning of this era of privacy invasion. Cell phones are only a decade old at this point, and will only become more powerful. There is no easy solution. You will be tracked. Adopting privacy and security technology is only a piece of the solution. Even then, reactionary, defensive techniques will work only as long as your adversary does not create a new tracking method. In the escalating arms race of digital tracking and surveillance, you will inevitably lose if you play by their rules.

Anonymity & Research

"To me, the magic word is consequences, consequences, consequences. It's just getting the word out that this may be the highest-stakes, highest-risk crossroads decision in your professional life. Nothing will ever be the same after this. And this is not something that you stroll into casually. It's something that requires as much or more planning than any test you've ever taken, because it's gonna be a test of your life."

—Tom Devine, Legal Director, Government Accountability Project

By standing up to power and exposing the truth, you can do a lot of good. You can save an organization millions of dollars. You can expose a culture of harassment. You can protect the public's health. Yet those who speak up are largely viewed negatively and punished for doing so.

Disclosing sensitive information will not be easy.

The state of data tracking around the world by governments and companies makes it nearly impossible to stand up to power without being immediately compromised through your digital information. If a company, a government, or an individual with $300 can track your every move, how will you expose the truth without being retaliated against immediately?[114]

Moreover, legal systems around the world tend to be set up to protect the Goliaths, not the Davids. So how can individuals safely approach changing systems and exposing the truth?

There is only one answer: be anonymous and do your homework first.

Your Identity

Protecting your identity is the priority, and anonymity is the key to success.

Anonymity is only possible when you can see yourself as the world does and then figure out how to disguise yourself.

Up to this point, you probably thought that the information you want to expose is the most important thing you have to protect. Wrong. Your identity must be protected above all else. If you don't protect your identity, you will be compromised, which can prevent you from exposing any information.

Your identity isn't defined by simply your name, birth date, Social Security number, or any other basic pieces of information. Your identity is not limited to how you identify internally and how you identify in terms of race or gender, but also how you express yourself in the world. You must view your identity as the rest of the world does. This includes how you are seen by governments, corporations, your social network, and even your family.

Data tracking and logging has evolved exponentially in the last few decades, and your identity is now bundled in numerous systems that are hard to even conceptualize.[115] Your identity now comprises an infinite number of data points, including the products and services you use, with whom you communicate, with whom your connections communicate, what you do online, and where you physically go.[116]

You are your habits.

The only real way to protect your identity is with anonymity. You must divest your true identity from the acts that you will perform that challenge power. The chances of retaliation are much lower if you are anonymous. Obviously, it is harder to be retaliated against if no one knows who you are. Anonymity can also correct the power imbalance between you and the system you are confronting. The underdog can have a fighting chance.

Danielle Brian, executive director of the Project on Government Oversight, emphasizes the importance of being unknown. "What you'll rarely see is the case of the person who isn't anonymous and seeing them walk away unscathed," she says.

As you proceed down the path of challenging the status quo and the powers that be, you may decide to be the public face of your cause. This can have benefits or drawbacks. But in order to have the choice to do so, rather than the obligation to do so, you must first be anonymous. If you aren't anonymous from the beginning, you will never get to decide if your identity will be made public. Instead, the decision will be out of your hands, and your identity will be at the mercy of your adversaries, the public, and perhaps the press.

So start by being anonymous. You can always decide to reveal your identity later on, but you can never get your anonymity back once your identity is revealed.

Anonymity and Reporting Harassment

If you have been harassed, you may feel that you can't be anonymous. The information you need to disclose (including who targeted you and the circumstances under which they did so) may seem too personal, too tightly wrapped up with your identity, to reveal anonymously. Don't fall into this trap. Protect your identity from the start, so you can strategically reveal it later on if needed.

Compartmentalization

Technology is continually changing, as new devices, apps, companies, and services released emerge on a daily basis. The digital tools you need to protect your identity are constantly in flux. It is even difficult for security professionals who have careers in technology to keep up with the latest best practices.

We are in a digital arms race. The surveillants have more time, money, and power. The only way to win this war is by adopting an alternative frame of mind: compartmentalization.

Compartmentalization draws from the world of information security, limiting who can access what and sharing information only on a "need-to-know basis." For example, inside government this might describe who has security clearance and who can view classified documents. In this instance, information is limited to a select group whose members have to be preapproved.

The more you can keep your activities compartmentalized and limit who knows what you are doing, the greater the chances that your identity will stay safe. Being anonymous means keeping your identity separate from any activities that challenge power.

Micah Lee, a technologist at *The Intercept* and a founder and board member of the Freedom of the Press Foundation, wrote that to compartmentalize, you must "Keep your whistleblowing activity as separate as possible from the rest of what you do." [117] [118]

For those who want to challenge power, compartmentalization means creating alternative identities for every situation, disconnecting them from one another. This way, if one alternative identity gets compromised, it doesn't reveal the others, especially your true identity. A simple example is to use a throwaway email account to contact a journalist in order to make sure your true identity isn't exposed.

There isn't a purely technological solution for compartmentalization. Compartmentalization is a mindset that focuses on anonymity and keeping your true identity separate from your actions. You should shift your focus from questions such as "How can I send a message securely?" to "How can I avoid disclosing my identity in this message?" Or even more generally, "How can I complete this action without linking it to my true identity?" This is the only strategy that can be used long-term to thwart surveillance.

Be thoughtful and be safe.

Pseudonymity

At some point you are going to need to communicate with others. This is usually the inflection point where things can really start to go wrong for someone trying to expose the truth. When someone inadvertently reveals their identity, the protection that anonymity offers is lost. A technique to combat this is pseudonymity, using an alternative identity. This allows your alternative identity to be compromised without affecting your real identity or your other identities.

To be pseudonymous simply means using a false name or alias. This can be done anonymously, where the false name is disconnected from any true identity, or in the case of many pen names used by authors, where the alias is an open secret where everyone knows the real identity. For your purposes, this means that instead of using your real name (or email, phone, username, et cetera), you use an alias or identifier that cannot be traced back to your real identity. Examples of this would be Citizen Four, one of

Edward Snowden's early handles; Satoshi Nakamoto, the alias used for the creator or creators of Bitcoin; and, of course, Deep Throat, the anonymous source critical to the *Washington Post*'s Watergate investigation. Compared to simply using an alias, these pseudonyms were never intended to be linked to someone's true identity.

To be clear, this isn't about having a fake ID. A fake ID still has your picture on it, linking your identity to the alias. This is about having a fake ID with no real information on it, and which is not connected to you in any way.

Some good examples of what not to do come from those who attempted to be anonymous to commit crimes and failed. Dread Pirate Roberts, the pseudonym for Ross Ulbricht, the creator of the Silk Road (an online black market for drugs), made a number of mistakes in trying to be anonymous. One in particular was buying nine different fake IDs, all of which had his real picture on them. The fake IDs were needed to rent servers online. By having his real face on the IDs, Ulbricht connected his identity to a crime. On top of it all, Ulbricht didn't need to have a real photo on the IDs in order to rent those servers, since the transaction would occur virtually, rather than in person.[119]

There are other reasons to use a pseudonym and disconnect your activities from your true identity. As Chris Walker from Tactical Technology Collective explains, "It's also about allowing you to continue to be a human being some of the time." Using these compartmentalization techniques alongside other alternative identities will allow you to maintain something closer to a normal life when you aren't challenging power.

So when using pseudonymous identities, keep them compartmentalized. Don't just separate them from your true identity, but disconnect them from your other anonymous alter egos as well. Protect each one just as you would your main identity. This will take time and forethought, but it's the best way you have to protect yourself while reaching out to others.

Uniqueness

Compartmentalization and anonymity aren't enough to keep you protected. There is the issue of unique acts that tie your identity to an action. For example, if you're walking down the street in a gorilla suit, no one can see your identity inside, but everyone sees you in the disguise. You are unique in this situation. You stick out in the crowd, and your behavior could give you away, even if your identity isn't known. The opposite of this is walking down the street in the same type of clothing everyone else around you is wearing.

Instead of wearing a gorilla suit, blend into the crowd and become hidden in plain sight.

Simply using software that promises anonymity can lead to trouble. A classic example of this is a Harvard student who called in a bomb threat anonymously online. When the network administrators at Harvard looked at the logs to see who had used a particular type of anonymization software that day, they saw that this software had only been used by one computer—the student's. The unique anonymization software made the student's computer stick out like a red flag on the network. Instead of thinking about how to hide in plain sight, the student just used anonymization software from his room on campus. Let's be clear: bomb threats are not a good thing, and this is not intended to advise you on how to get away with a bomb threat. Rather, this is a warning against misplaced trust in software that promises anonymity but doesn't really keep you safe.[120]

Another example of someone not focusing on hiding in plain sight comes from the Reality Winner saga. Reality Winner was an American military contractor who accessed, printed, and delivered to the media a classified NSA document that showed that Russian hackers had targeted and accessed a U.S. voting-software supplier. Winner made a number of mistakes in attempting to be anonymous, but in particular, she didn't consider how unique her actions might be.

The printing of documents is logged within most government systems, and it turned out that only six people with access to the report actually printed it. This immediately made her one of a handful of suspects, and it was easy enough to track her down.[121]

If your actions are unique and tied to your true identity, you will be identified. If you are the only one with access to a certain type of information, it will lead back to you. Concentrate on being hidden in plain sight and performing actions that could have been done by a multitude of individuals and not just you.

Focus on blending into the crowd. That's the best way not to be seen.

Privacy and Encryption

Privacy can be an aspect of how you obfuscate your information, but privacy isn't anonymity. Often, the word "privacy" is used to denote who can see what. On Twitter, for example, you can make your tweets *private* instead of *public*. This means someone must be approved to be able to see your tweets, ostensibly giving you control over your Twitter account. In reality, this ostensible control doesn't lessen the connection between your identity and your Twitter account. If you don't anonymize the way you create your account, what you post, and how you post it, you will still be using your own Twitter account.

Anonymity (or in this case pseudonymity), on the other hand, means being able to control a digital account that is not linked in any way to your true identity. Many activists around the world use anonymous Twitter accounts to amplify their voices without their opinions being associated with their real identities. They aren't generally using "private" Twitter accounts; they are using public accounts, but they are using them anonymously, so that their message can be heard by all without identifying the person spreading it.[122]

If you want to establish an anonymous Twitter account, finish reading this chapter and then do more anonymous research. For instance, check out the guides by Micah Lee and The Grugq.[123] [124]

Sometimes people also substitute the term *encryption* for anonymity. But encryption is simply a method of encoding information: a tool to store, send, and receive information securely. It is not identity protection. Paul Manafort notably made the mistake of assuming that whatever he typed into the encrypted messaging application WhatsApp on his phone was private because it used encryption. With a routine court order, the FBI was able to retrieve backups on iCloud of Manafort's unencrypted chat log messages, which suggested that he had attempted witness tampering.[125] As Manafort perhaps learned, encryption is a method for coding information, and applications are mere tools for doing this. Encryption methods can help limit the exposure of one's identity; but, by itself, encryption is not a holistic system of protection.

Encryption is the method of encoding readable information (plaintext) into coded information (ciphertext), such that without a key to unlock the coded message, the information is indecipherable. Though we may not realize it, we use encryption every day on many of our devices and apps. For example, website URLs that start with HTTPS instead of HTTP are "secured," meaning the communication transmitted between the server and the browser is encrypted. When you log in to a website that's using HTTPS, your password and communication will be encrypted and sent to the server as a coded message, making it nearly impossible for eavesdroppers to discover your password in transit.[126]

In general, encryption can be divided up into two general forms: symmetric encryption, where the same key is used to encode and decode information, and asymmetric encryption, where two keys are used, one to encrypt and another to decrypt. An example of symmetric encryption would be encrypting a hard drive or a document with a password, with the same password used to lock and unlock the data. Symmetric encryption is almost always implemented in cases of a single user safely storing information with a password. On the other hand, asymmetric encryption is almost always implemented for communication purposes, such as encrypted email and the other privacy-focused messaging applications recommended in this book. In these cases, the sender uses one key to encrypt the message and the receiver uses another to decrypt it, though in these systems the user isn't entering a password every time an encoded message is received. Rather, the software handles the encryption and decryption. This is one reason why it is often difficult to know if you are actually using an encrypted communication method.

Often, both encrypted and unencrypted communication systems look the same to the user. Take for example the difference between using regular text-messaging and using Apple iMessage (which is encrypted but not recommended for the purposes in this book). To the user, the messages on the phone look exactly the same, but the regular text messages are transmitted across cellular networks in plaintext (unencoded), whereas the iMessage communications are transmitted in ciphertext (encoded).[127] An eavesdropper intercepting data moving across the network would be able to read the text messages but not the iMessages.

Though encrypted communication systems are clearly beneficial to users, adoption of them has lagged. One reason for the lack of adoption is a general education problem: people often don't know or understand the benefits of using them. Another reason is that technology developers don't always build in encrypted systems by default, or more commonly, they don't make it apparent to the user when they are using an encrypted system. Consider the lock icon in the top left corner of your web browser, which is present to signify to the user that HTTPS (encryption) is used on a website. Many users assume that the symbol means that a site is secure or safe, neither of which is intrinsically true. Even a site using HTTPS could deliver malware, a virus, or a phishing attack against a user. The only thing that a user can be sure of with HTTPS is that the information transmitted to the server is encrypted across the network.[128]

Make sure your phone and computer have device encryption turned on. For phones, this means turning it on in the settings (though a lot of phones come with it enabled by default). For computers, you'll want to turn on hard drive encryption in the settings. For each of these devices, including your phones, you must use a strong password (or PIN or swipe pattern, depending on the system). Otherwise, all the encryption in the world won't matter if someone can simply turn on your device and start looking around. "Password security is very important," says Mar Cabra, who was head of the Data & Research Unit at the International Consortium of Investigative Journalists during the Panama Papers story. "If your phone-code is 1111 or 1234, it doesn't matter if you are using end-to-end encryption." Be responsible for your own digital safety as you are configuring your devices, especially when you are choosing a password. Make sure to pick a strong one.

Practical Anonymity

You walk out of your house and get in your car. You enter the address of a big box store into Google Maps and follow the directions on your phone to the store. You walk around the store for a while and end up talking with a salesperson for a few minutes about different pay-as-you-go "burner" phones. You find the one that sounds right for you and go to the checkout and buy it with a credit card. You get back in your car and drive home.

In this example of buying a burner cell phone, what isn't anonymous? What data could tie you to the act of simply buying a phone? The phone? Google Maps? Your credit-card company? A license plate reader? The salesperson?

Overwhelming, right? Anonymity may seem difficult to achieve, but by concentrating on the mindset rather than the details it will get easier. Let's start with payments.

Cash

The most obvious and easiest technique for buying things anonymously is using cash. It has the potential to leave no transactional traces. A credit card, on the other hand, can leave a clear trail of data with your bank and the store's point of sale system.

The only real problem with cash is that you might still be connected to the transaction in other ways. You could be recognized at the store, captured on video, tracked via cell phone, leave latent prints on the bills, or somehow have a bill's serial numbers traced.

Consider where you get your cash. Is it directly from an ATM where the bill's serial numbers could be connected to you? Better to get the cash in larger bills, then get change—including smaller bills—during a standard register transaction, and then use that money elsewhere. Perhaps this is overkill, but it's better to be safe.

When buying things in person, go to places that you don't usually frequent. This will make it less likely that you will run into someone you know or that someone will recognize you. It will also make it harder for you to be identified if someone comes looking. Attempt to be as forgettable as possible and limit the amount that digital systems or surveillance systems can record you.

Also, limit your digital data trail when purchasing items anonymously. Never bring your own personal phone with you when buying things anonymously. Doing so can leave location data on your phone, on carrier servers, on retailer servers, and potentially on government servers, noting where you have been and when.

Leave other digital devices such as fitness trackers or GPS enabled watches at home. They can also generate location information, such as where you've been and when. Devices with

Wi-Fi, Bluetooth, RFID, or NFC can potentially be scanned and tracked, too, so don't bring them with you, or put them in a signal-blocking pouch.

You may be surprised to know that most passports have an RFID chip inside of them, making them scannable within a few meters. The same applies to security cards and other electronic identification cards. Don't bring them with you.

Going on foot or biking to a store is usually your best option. Public transport can leave copies of your face on cameras. License plate readers are becoming quite common in parking lots, and some cities have license plate reader vehicles that patrol and record, making cars a potential data point that can be traced. In the end, the transportation method that leaves the smallest data trail will be your best choice.

Always wear clothing that masks your identity. This could be clothing that is bulky and hides your face, like a hooded sweatshirt and baggy jeans. It might seem ridiculous, but in some instances a disguise is actually a reasonable option. A hat and sunglasses are a great way to make face detection and recognition harder.

Above all else, be sure to wear clothing that blends in with those around you. A cowboy outfit in the middle of New York City might be more conspicuous than any disguise. You must fit into the crowd and be easily forgettable by those who see you.

Plastic

A second common method for anonymous purchasing is to use a prepaid Mastercard or Visa gift card. These can come in handy at places that don't accept cash or when purchasing services online where cash isn't an option.

When buying prepaid gift cards, be sure that you pay for them in cash and buy them in smaller values, like $25 or $50 maximum. Higher-value cards and variable-value cards often need to be registered online—which you do not want to do. Of course, registration of these cards can be done with a fake name and address, but they should also be done using an anonymous internet connection (covered later in this book).[129] Registering cards is dangerous unless done right. It creates another potential data point that could compromise your identity. Only buy prepaid gift cards with cash, and use the previously detailed techniques for their purchase.

When using a prepaid gift card to pay for services online, it is a good idea to test it first. For example, if you're buying a service like an email account with a gift card over Tor, buy it, then wait a week to make sure your account isn't deactivated because of "fraudulent activity."

Cryptocurrencies

Another way to pay for things anonymously is to use cryptocurrencies. They are the main currency used on the dark web, and with some cryptocoins it is possible to send money anonymously.

Cryptocurrencies like Zcash are built to offer privacy and anonymity. Look for services that accept one of these or another anonymity-focused cryptocurrency rather than going through the process of acquiring other coins anonymously.

Unfortunately, most cryptocurrencies like Bitcoin and Etherium cannot be bought or transferred anonymously. To solve this, you need to use a laundering service or to find a seller (typically on the dark web) who will sell you cryptocurrencies anonymously.

None of the ways of anonymously buying cryptocurrency are trivial, and most methods take time and practice to do them consistently and securely. This process also has a major downside: if done incorrectly, it can easily leave a connection between your true identity and an anonymous one. Be careful if you explore these pathways, and do more research.

A wealth of knowledge exists on cryptocurrency, especially on the dark web. Do your homework and use cash or a prepaid card to acquire cryptocurrency if you can.

Note that transfers of Bitcoin cannot be reversed, so it's especially important to triple-check addresses and amounts before you confirm.

Practice this stuff in real life. It will help you look at the world through the lens of anonymity and get you into the mindset of compartmentalization. You need to break your normal habits and learn how not to leave traces of your identity lying around.

This is the first step in preparing to expose the truth.

Anonymous Research

Consider just how important being able to read, think, and prepare to expose the truth without anyone knowing might be to:

- a young immigrant trying to research possible avenues to citizenship;
- someone questioning their sexual orientation in a country where non-heterosexual relationships are not accepted;
- a mother in an abusive relationship, trying to find support and pathways to safety.

The goal is to find answers without revealing that you're conducting research. You may not want the government, an employer, or even your family or friends to know what you're researching.

In less digital times this might have meant going to a library in disguise to read anonymously. For better or worse, research is now often reliant on access to the internet. So knowing how to gain access anonymously is crucial. Unfortunately, getting on the web securely and without being tracked is no easy feat. There is no bulletproof solution. Instead you must adopt an anonymous mindset, so that even if the tools and techniques change, you can adjust your thinking and create a new safe way to conduct research.

By learning anonymous research techniques you will become empowered to dig deeper into the ideas in this book, to verify that the suggested methods throughout this book are indeed the best practices, and to give yourself greater protection against unknown threats.

Looking at information without anyone knowing you're accessing it—such as browsing the web anonymously—is the most basic form of anonymity. We often forget this truth. Just searching Google from your phone or home computer creates a myriad of logs that governments and corporations can use to track your every click.

By browsing anonymously, you can make it so that those data trails can't be connected to your true identity. Think of anonymous web browsing as being able to read a book at home: no one knows you have the book or that you are reading it (depending on how you have procured the book). The information and its transmission are secure.

There are three main ways to do research anonymously:

1. Go to a location such as a library and use a computer there anonymously. Make sure you use Incognito mode or private browsing in the web browser.
2. Reboot a normal computer into the operating system Tails using a bootable USB stick, then use its prepackaged Tor browser to surf the web anonymously.
3. Create your own anonymous tablet and use it at a Wi-Fi location that you don't use in your normal life.

Using Someone Else's Computer

When you're going to the library or any location with computers to use anonymously, consider how you will get there and how you will gain access while limiting the data points you leave behind.

Who sees you? With whom must you interact? What surveillance systems will record you? Will your license plate be tracked? Do you have cash to pay for things? Should you consider wearing a disguise? Is your clothing too unique? Are you going to need to register or otherwise provide identification to access a computer?

These are all reasonable questions to ask. The more you consider how you are surveilled offline and online, the more you will be able to blend into the crowd and go undetected. Remember to leave your regular phone behind whenever you are attempting to do things anonymously.

Your phone is a snitch. Leave it at home. The library you go to should not be close to your home. Hopefully no one will recognize you there. If possible, walk or bike. Anything that leaves fewer traces of your movements is better.

Once you're online, do not do anything you would normally do online. Don't log in to a non-anonymous account. Don't log in to your regular email account. Don't log in to Facebook.

Keep all your anonymous activities separate from your normal habits. Do not check your favorite blog or news site, and never log in to any site with your true identity. Leave no connections between what you do online anonymously and what you do normally on the internet. Be smart and cautious. Think before you act.

TAILS: The Amnesiac Operating System

If using a computer in the library anonymously doesn't feel secure enough, consider another suggested means of connecting to the internet anonymously: by using a special USB thumb drive to reboot your normal computer or a library computer into the operating system Tails.

Tails is an acronym for The Amnesic Incognito Live System, and it's the choice of many whistleblowers and those trying to remain anonymous in difficult scenarios. Edward Snowden successfully used the Tails operating system to compartmentalize his communications with journalists.

The Tails operating system is based on Linux, which is a free and open-source operating system. It has a few key features that make it completely different than Windows, macOS, or other flavors of Linux.

Tails is built specifically for safeguarding anonymity and privacy, and it accomplishes this in a few interesting ways. It is an amnesiac system, meaning that by default, the operating system saves nothing as you use it, and each time you boot up you start from a blank slate. During shutdown or whenever the USB drive is removed from the computer, Tails attempts to clean up after itself so that even a sophisticated adversary can't recover any data pertaining to what the user was doing.

Security-wise, Tails is configured to send all network traffic through the Tor network.

Tor

Tor is both a network and a web browser. It works by sending your web traffic around the world through randomized routes of computers within the Tor network. Through a special networking protocol, Tor enables your web browsing to be close to anonymous. This means you can use it to anonymously visit a website like Reddit and start searching for more information on how to be anonymous online. Reddit's servers won't know who you are, and anyone observing the network traffic, such as the library's internet provider or the NSA, will be kept from knowing both who you are and what website you are visiting. For example, the library's ISP (Internet Service Provider) might know that you are using Tor, but it wouldn't know that you are visiting Reddit. And an NSA server might be able to see that someone is visiting Reddit, but it wouldn't know that it is you.

Of course, this only works if you are simply viewing websites and not logging onto them. For example, if you log in to your personal email through Tor, your browsing may no longer be anonymous. So only view sites anonymously or use anonymous online accounts through this connection.

Generally speaking, if you use the Tor Browser and don't modify it at all, if you don't enable Javascript, and if you don't log in to any websites, you can assume that your browsing is anonymous. There are always caveats, however, so please do more research to see where things stand currently.

Tails is quite different than just using the Tor Browser on a Mac or Windows computer. In those cases, the Tor Browser is focused solely on anonymizing your web-browsing. While you're using the Tails system, though, any connection to the internet, whether it's from an email application or a chat program, flows through the Tor network. This enables an even greater level of anonymity, obscuring even your connection to fetch your mail.

Tails also has a number of useful built-in tools: the Metadata Anonymisation Toolkit, KeePassX password manager, and open-source software for image and video editing.

One of the biggest obstacles to using Tails is creating the initial USB stick. This can seem daunting. Those who aren't as tech-savvy might be inclined to avoid this, but it isn't actually too hard to do. To make a Tails USB, follow the instructions at https://tails.boum.org/install.

Have a computer ready and two 32 GB USB sticks on hand (8 GB is the minimum required, but extra space never hurts). Go step-by-step. If need be, print out the instructions or keep them on a tablet or phone, so you can read them while you work. If you find the instructions overwhelming, seek out a local trustworthy techie for advice.

Once you have a working Tails USB, plug it into a computer and restart it, holding down the key or key combination that makes the computer boot from USB (this will differ on various computers, so look up how to do this on the particular machine you're using).

Once you have a copy of Tails up and running, it is no trouble to make a new USB stick to give to someone else. While you're using Tails, simply connect another USB stick to the computer and use the Tails Installer tool to clone the USB stick. This is by far the best method for creation and distribution. You can follow the cloning instructions here: https://tails.boum.org/install/linux/clone-overview.

One last note on Tails: it is important to keep the Tails operating system up to date. This can be done by creating a new USB installation from scratch or by downloading the newest copy of Tails (in the form of an ISO file), then installing it onto a blank USB stick via the same Tails Installer program. Tails will notify you if a new version is available when it starts up.

Finding Trustworthy Tech Assistance

Of course, not everyone reading this book will have a high level of technical knowledge. If you don't, it's OK. Take your time and be mindful of your actions. If you get stuck, do more research first. Failing that, consider who you can reach out to from an anonymous email account to ask for help. If it really comes down to it, consider who you know that might be able to help you and reach out to them. Be careful, and decide whether it's possible to work with them without revealing your intentions.

Tablets

The other way of doing anonymous research is to set up an anonymous Android tablet, one that's bought with cash and that has never been online at your home, your office, or anywhere else you normally go.

When buying a tablet, get a small one. Tablets with 7-inch screens look an awful lot like large phones, which can be useful in two ways:

1. This makes it look like you are just using a phone out-side a building when you are actually using its Wi-Fi anonymously.

2. If you ever need to take photos anonymously, it's bet-ter to be using a device that looks like a phone rather than a tablet. You can conceal it more easily and go unnoticed.

Unlike smartphones, most tablets typically do not have embed-ded GPS or baseband microchips. A tablet without such chips can't automatically leak location information to a provider or to applications that would have access to GPS or cell signal. Tablets aren't perfect (Wi-Fi can still be used to determine your location), but they are more secure than smartphones.

Take your tablet to a location that has free Wi-Fi. Make sure that this is somewhere away from your usual routines. This can be a coffee shop, a public library, or even a McDonald's.

When using free Wi-Fi, remember that if it doesn't require a password, it isn't secure. Without a password to join a network, the connection between the tablet and the Wi-Fi router will flow unencrypted. This makes it possible for someone at the coffee shop on the same unsecured Wi-Fi network to eavesdrop on all of your unencrypted network traffic.

This is a reasonable time to remind you that if you are visiting websites that don't require HTTPS, any data between you and the website is unencrypted, allowing anyone along the communication flow to eavesdrop on you.

Fortunately, eavesdropping doesn't need to be a huge concern. With this tablet, we will be focused on using software that by default encrypts everything, making eavesdropping nearly impossible. When you're first setting up any anonymous device, do it from an anonymous internet connection. Never use your anonymous tablet at home!

Decline everything the device offers, as far as connecting to things automatically. Don't accept other software installations. Don't send Google feedback or logs automatically. Don't connect to Wi-Fi yet, and skip setting up a Google account for the time being.

Settings

Before we do anything else, we want to make sure location tracking is turned off. You can find this under "Settings > Privacy > Location." Turn location tracking off.

Please note that throughout the tablet settings section, we will provide likely names of the settings you should update, but these menus are specific to each device and the Android operating system version that it uses. You will need to find the right settings on your own device. Use this as a guide, but use your own judgement for your specific context.

The next thing to do is to set a strong password for the device under "Settings > Security > Lock Screen." Change the screen lock type to password, and if you have the option available, turn on "Require password to turn on device." When choosing a password, try something at least 12 characters long and unique. It's best to use a passphrase for this, consisting of multiple words, to ensure that this password is difficult to guess or crack (see the discussion of diceware passphrase generation in the subsequent "Passphrases" section for one method of generating this type of password). There will not be a backup for this password, so you will need to memorize it *now*.

You should also make sure that any facial recognition or fingerprint scanning settings are turned off. Look for biometric settings under "Lock Screen." Note: These are newer features that are usually associated with more expensive devices, so you might not see these on yours.

Under "Lock Screen Preferences," choose "Don't show notifications at all" on the lock screen.

Next up is to encrypt your device. How this is handled greatly depends on the Android version installed on your device. In earlier Android versions, full disk encryption could be turned on under "Settings > Lock Screen" and "Security > Other Security Settings > Encrypt Device." With newer devices, Google has shifted to a file-based encryption method that is less transparent to the user. You will need to do more research on your particular device to figure out how to enable encryption if possible. Some devices now come with encryption turned on by default. For others, you can only encrypt your device by enabling "Developer Options," and then turning on encryption. Please do more homework to be sure you're updating the correct settings to encrypt your device. Encryption is important!

The other thing we want to turn off is your keyboard's predictive typing. If we don't, the keyboard will learn your anonymous email addresses and other data you type in that could give away your identity if the tablet ever fell into the wrong hands. To address this, go to your keyboard settings under "Settings > Languages & Input." The exact settings available will depend on your brand of tablet and the version of the operating system that it uses, but you'll want to go through all keyboard settings and look for anything involving "smart typing," "predictive text," "next-word suggestions," "personalized suggestions," "share snippets," or anything else like that, and turn it off.

Depending on your need for assistive speech-to-text and text-to-speech, you should also disable as many voice and Google Assistant settings as possible. The less your microphone can listen to you, the better. Along these lines, it's likely a good practice to ensure "Now Playing" is also disabled on your device if this is available on your operating-system version, since this enables the microphone to capture sound data around you even when your device is locked.

Passphrases, Not Passwords

When you first connect the tablet to Wi-Fi, your first point of business should be to install a password manager. This way you can keep track of all the various anonymous accounts and passwords that you create.

Unfortunately, you can't install applications on the tablet without a Google account (there are ways around this, but not only are they are too cumbersome for this manual, they also reduce the security of your tablet—if you want to try this type of thing, search the internet for "sideload Android app").

Go to the Play Store and you will be prompted to create a new account. When choosing a username, try creating one in another language, which is an easy red herring. Memorize the password for the moment. You will soon enter it into a password manager for safekeeping.

I have had success with the Android application Keepass2Android, which is a free password manager. Other password managers are out there, such as KeePassDroid. KeePass in general is an open-source standard for password managers, and Keepass2Android is a nice implementation of this standard for Android.

Install Keepass2Android from the Play Store and set a strong password for the manager. You can now store the password for the Google account you have created in this password manager.

You should immediately memorize two passwords: 1) the password you use to log in to the tablet and 2) the password to unlock the password manager on the tablet.

Most of us have been taught that adding symbols and numbers to passwords will make them strong, but what really strengthens a password is its length. Generate a password from a phrase of multiple words strung together, instead of a single word, and you will make it exponentially stronger. Let's start by referring to these types of passwords as passphrases.

Diceware is a technique for creating random passphrases that are relatively easy to memorize, while also long enough to be nearly impossible for a computer to crack with brute-force methods. Here are the basics.

Start with a word list of approximately 8,000 words, where each word is numbered from 11,111 to 66,666. You can download a word list from the Electronic Frontier Foundation here: https://www.eff.org/dice/.

Then roll five dice at once, giving you a random number, say 12,451. This number will correspond to a word in the list, which will be the first part of your passphrase. By repeating this process at least six times, you will generate a passphrase that will be nearly impossible for today's computers to crack.

An example of a passphrase that might be generated by this technique would be "AnyhowCableRemovingPunkSensually-Blank." It consists of six individual words that combine to make one random, long, and strong passphrase.

Random words are much harder to crack than words that have connections or associations with your family, childhood, or life in general.

Make your own randomized passphrases. Make a different one for each of your devices.

Securing Your Connection

When you normally connect to the internet via Wi-Fi, your data will pass through the Wi-Fi base station or router, the modem, ISP servers, and any other servers between your computer and the final server that you are visiting. With your data going through all of these intermediaries, it could be monitored in a variety of ways. To limit the data that an ISP or a strong adversary like the NSA could capture about you, we will secure your connection to the internet.

This can be done in two main ways, either with Tor or with a VPN. Please read up on both here and decide, depending on your adversary and situation, which you will primarily use for your device. In most cases I recommend Tor instead of a VPN service, because it offers better protection.

You should be aware that in some cases, for instance if very few people on a network are using it, Tor can make your device stick out like a sore thumb, allowing your network administrator to more easily flag your device. Even if they do so, however, they likely won't be able to know what you are viewing. So it's highly worth considering.

Tor

To secure your network connection with Tor on a tablet, you will need to install Orbot and the Tor Browser from the Google Play Store. Orbot acts similarly to a VPN, routing traffic from other applications through the Tor network instead of directly to the internet. When you first open Orbot, you will need to turn on "VPN Mode," which allows traffic from all applications to flow through Tor.

To start the connection to the Tor network, tap the start button in Orbot, which is the big onion button in the center. It may take a little while to connect, but once it says "NOTICE: Bootstrapped 100%: Done" all the traffic from your device will go through the

Tor network. To browse the web anonymously, go back to your device's home screen and select the Tor Browser icon.

Beware: the landscape of Tor-enabled applications on Android is changing. The new Tor Browser was released only recently, allowing it to be used independently of Orbot. By itself, Tor Browser will anonymize your web browsing, but it will not protect the other applications on your device. If you do need everything protected, either combine Tor Browser with Orbot or use it with VPN. Do more research, as these recommendations are ever-evolving.

Tor can also be used to visit hidden services, a.k.a. the dark web. The dark web actually consists of anonymous websites hosted on computers within the Tor network. These websites only work within the Tor Browser, and can't be accessed from the regular internet or a regular web browser. You can always tell a site is on the dark web if the URL ends in ".onion" and has a long string of characters before it, such as http://kpvz7ki2v5agwt35.onion.

The dark web is useful in a few ways: 1) other anonymity-focused individuals have put resources there, and 2) If you want to do anything with anonymous cryptocurrencies, the dark web has lots of information on anonymity and other advice for protecting yourself.

Some good jumping-off points for trying to find websites on the dark web are:

- the onions page on Reddit (https://www.reddit.com/r/onions);
- searching for "dark web links 2018" on Pastebin (https://pastebin.com), e.g., "The Hidden Wiki," which is a good starting point for exploration; and

- Ahmia, a search engine for hidden services, which at the time of writing was located at http://msydqstlz-2kzerdg.onion/.

Nothing on the dark web is completely straightforward, and it might feel closer to the internet in 1998 than today. But take your time and don't worry. Use common sense and you'll be fine exploring it.

VPN

Virtual private networks (VPNs) originated as a way for remote employees to securely tunnel their network connection back to their companies' headquarters. This essentially allows remote computers to connect to the internal network of an organization as if they are still physically inside the building.

VPNs became popular with internet users because they can associate your traffic with an IP address that's tied to a physical address in another city or country, obfuscating your true location. This can circumvent government firewalls and company blocks on location-locked content. With a VPN, people in the United States can make it look as if they are located in the United Kingdom, for instance, to gain full access to the BBC's content.

This isn't a foolproof system, mostly because you need to trust your VPN not to reveal your information to other parties. In essence, with a VPN, you shift trust in your internet connection from your internet service provider to the VPN provider. The advantage of a VPN is that the VPN will encrypt all of the information from your computer until it reaches the VPN's server.

This makes it harder for those in physical proximity to you (e.g., others in your Wi-Fi café) or those who might intercept traffic at a country-level internet gateway (e.g., the government of another country) to gain access to your data.

Choosing a VPN provider can be difficult. Try an internet search for "VPN." A vast array of services are available, each with its own pros and cons. Look through review sites that compare and contrast services offered, but beware of fake review sites that are really just pushing a particular VPN. This is no easy task. Check out the Freedom of the Press Foundation's recommendation here: https://freedom.press/training/choosing-a-vpn/

I have had good luck with the VPN service provider "Private Internet Access" (PIA). One particularly great feature of this service is that it can be paid for anonymously with a Starbucks gift card. Other brands of gift cards are also accepted, but Starbucks has worked well for me, because it is so ubiquitous.

To set up PIA, go to https://www.privateinternetaccess.com and scroll down until you see the option to "Pay anonymously with many major brand gift cards." Then enter a new anonymous email address that you created just for this service, and then enter the number of the Starbucks gift card that you purchased with cash at a random location.

PIA will then email your username and password to the anonymous address that you entered. Download the VPN by Private Internet Access application from the Google Play Store and log in with the provided username and password. Store this username and password in your password manager for safekeeping.

Now, any time you connect to a Wi-Fi network, you should immediately open the PIA app and connect to its network. By default, PIA is configured so that all of your applications' traffic runs through the PIA VPN system. In effect, you now have better encryption when using Wi-Fi.

While you're using the VPN, use a privacy-focused browser such as Firefox Focus or DuckDuckGo Privacy Browser instead of the Google Chrome browser that comes packaged with the tablet. This will leave fewer traces and won't connect your browsing to the Google email identity you created while trying to configure the tablet.

Risk Assessment

"I think that whistleblowers who go to the press do incredibly brave and important things... But for their safety, it's important that they fully understand the consequences of what they're doing, and that it can often be very risky, and that even if you do everything 'right,' it's possible to get caught."

—Trevor Timm, Executive Director, Freedom of the Press Foundation

It should be obvious by now: when planning to disclose, consider your safety in a careful and systematic way. We have emphasized anonymity as the basic mindset for doing research and disclosing information. The specifics of how you work within this anonymous structure can be clarified through doing a risk assessment. The term "threat modeling" is often used to describe this process in the field of information technology and our suggestions have taken cues from that. But we will also draw from other analogous processes, such as risk analysis and security planning.

Threat modeling usually involves making a diagram showing where and how data is stored, accessed, and transferred, whether in databases, on computers, in the cloud, etc. The idea is to see how all the systems connect and then identify vulnerable points that could be exploited. This process works well for digital systems. But the stakes, risks, and assets are different for whistleblowers and those who seek to challenge power with the truth. So instead of exclusively using the IT threat modeling methodology, we will look toward processes designed for human rights activists. We will use the term "risk assessment," relying on models that are less focused on just digital information.

No matter what we call it, all of these systems share the same basic four components: identifying 1) who or what is a threat, 2) what you are trying to protect, 3) how that threat could manifest, and 4) its potential impacts. Then you can evaluate the possible scenarios, prioritize them, and make plans accordingly. Nobody can eliminate all the dangers, but you can certainly reduce your risks.

"It's like deciding where to park your car and whether or not to leave your bag in the car, or put it in the trunk, or bring it with you," says Ken Montenegro, director of information technology at Asian Americans Advancing Justice–Los Angeles. "You are making a judgment of what you consider to be safe based on your circumstances and what you think someone will likely do in a certain situation."

For those attempting to disclose information, the dangers aren't limited to digital threats. You may face legal, social, psychological, or even physical threats, with the specifics depending heavily on your own particular situation. Someone who witnesses a systematic danger to public safety inside a drug company may face a much different set of threats than someone who uncovers embezzlement by the boss at a nonprofit organization. An undocumented worker who is being sexually harassed at her place of business will face a different set of risks than a citizen who is sexually harassed within the media industry. While the threats and risks will vary, one thing will be consistent among almost all situations: a power imbalance between you and the individuals, the organization, or the systems you are up against, David versus Goliath.

RISK ASSESSMENT

To practice risk assessment, consider the following scenarios:

1. A corporate employee at an energy company has taken internal confidential reports home and is considering sending them to a watchdog environmental group. If the fact that the documents were taken from work is discovered, the employee could be not only fired but also potentially sued by the company for stealing company property. This individual needs to decide if they are willing to risk the legal battle and subsequent fines or go to jail if found guilty.

2. An employee of a small startup company has been witness to sexual harassment by one of the founders of the company, though they haven't been harassed themselves. There is no human resources department. The employee would like to tell the world publicly about what goes on inside this organization, but is concerned about revealing their identity, as well as whether the individuals who were harassed would want to be identified. They worry about repercussions for themselves and those who were harassed.

3. A public employee in law enforcement is considering talking to a reporter about internal systematic discrimination in the workplace. If their identity is discovered, the individual could find themselves isolated from their community. Without the support of their coworkers, they risk being effectively blacklisted from their industry or never getting a promotion.

4. A guest worker from India is in the United States with an H-1B visa and is being contracted to a large tech firm by the visa broker that brought them to the United States. The visa broker is threatening to sue if the worker leaves the company to seek employment elsewhere. The worker is considering going to the press, but worries about retaliation, including having their visa revoked or wages withheld.

Next, to create a risk assessment for these scenarios or for your own situation that you may be facing, work through the following questions. Research your answers anonymously to gather more information. Be as specific as possible in your answers. Consider of course where you write your answers down, and safely store your answers or destroy them.

Who doesn't want you to disclose this information? Who is your adversary?

List all of the possibilities: individuals, organizations, corporations, governments, even an entire industry. In some cases, such as the reporting of sexual harassment or assault, there may be other victims. Do they want to be revealed? Who could be harmed by your disclosure?

What do you have that your adversary wants? What are your assets?

Your identity should be your number one asset, but also list any related notes you've taken: emails, devices, recorded or written communications, digital or physical documents, images or photos, videos, location data, lab test results, medical records, or even the names of individuals or partners that you have contacted. This can also include alliances or relationships you've made, including the identity of people in your support network, victims, money, or the research you've conducted.

How can your adversary gain access to your assets? What methods do they have and how far will they go?

Consider not only technical or software methods (such as access to your email, access logs for files, or lists of URLs you've visited), but also legal or even social ways they could identify you or gain access to your assets. Possible answers include security cameras, spyware, subpoenas, blackmail (are there skeletons in your closet?), tipping off law enforcement to search your property, and hiring security firms to track you. Will they try to isolate you socially? Demote you? Don't assume that your adversary has the same ethics that you do. This is likely your first time doing this, but has your adversary been through this before? What might an unethical adversary be able to find out about you or blame on you?

What are the consequences if your adversary succeeds, and specifically for whom?

Could you go to jail? Lose your job? Be deported? Be physically harmed? Lose respect in your industry? Will it be hard on your family? Could anyone else you care about be targeted? What do your partners stand to lose? Will you be sued? Might there be monetary consequences if you lose? How long might these consequences reverberate? Keep in mind that even if your adversary is not fully successful, their investigative efforts can still put you through the wringer and make your life difficult and compartmentalized for a long time. In some cases, "success" for your adversary may simply be to tie you up in court, cast doubt on your professional reputation, or make your workplace experience so miserable that you leave. These are potential consequences to consider in your list.

Now take all of these specific threats and rank them. Consider the magnitude of risk, as well as what's probable versus what's possible. What's the biggest risk or danger? What's the most likely? Decide the important ones to address in your plans. More long-shot and generalized threats should be deprioritized, and more likely and impactful ones should be prioritized. For example, consider this threat: "If a hacker finds a vulnerability in the Android operating system that exposes all passwords, my adversary will be able to access my materials." This is both unlikely and would affect everyone, not just you, so it can be deprioritized. Alternatively, a threat such as "If my boss finds out about my emails with a journalist, I will be fired" is specific, carries a high magnitude of risk, and is very probable, so it should be highly prioritized. Concentrate on specific threats that are probable.

From this list of threats you can create a security plan. This plan should focus on ways to 1) increase capacities, which are protocols, tools, systems, or ways of operating that decrease the likelihood that a threat will occur; and 2) decrease vulnerabilities, which are gaps in how you currently operate that make it more likely that a threat will occur. All of the items in your security plan should be specific.

A good plan might include things like:

- Only communicate with a partner using encrypted messaging on your pseudonymous phone so that communication won't be logged on your personal phone, which would make it easier to subpoena.

- Only travel by public transport when going to meet with your lawyer and leave your phone at home so that it will be harder for someone to follow you or connect you to your lawyer.
- Never use your work computer to do research on safe ways to disclose information.
- Keep a journal at home with times and dates of everything related to your efforts. This way you have a form of evidence, should you ever need it.

As you continue on with this book, be sure to come back to review and build upon your risk assessment. This isn't something you do once and then it's done. You must work on it regularly so that it stays up to date. Be sure to review your threat model and security plan at regular intervals. As you plan, keep in mind that things will change.

Whether you are ready to disclose information or not, whether you are just starting to research anonymously, or whether you are currently communicating with someone else securely, make sure that you consider all of your assets. You and your identity are your greatest assets. Protect them at all costs.

The key is to consider these risks as early as possible in the process of exposing the truth and in a systematic way, avoiding some of the obvious traps. Above all else, keep a clear head and "trust your gut instincts," says Chloe Caras, whose exposure of "extraordinary" sexual harassment led to a settlement and the bankruptcy of celebrity Mike Isabella's restaurant group in D.C. in 2018.[130] Be systematic in your thinking and your consideration of the risks, but trust yourself. If something feels unsafe, it's best to listen to that feeling.

If you want to dive further into creating a risk assessment, Front Line Defenders, a nonprofit group that supports human rights defenders, has a very practical guide: *Workbook on Security: Practical Steps for Human Rights Defenders at Risk* (https://www. frontlinedefenders.org/en/resource-publication/workbook-security-practical-steps-human-rights-defenders-risk). You might not be working internationally or working on human rights, but this workbook can help you think more broadly about security and risks than many IT-focused threat models. Do your homework and be prepared. This will be a long battle. Protect yourself from the very beginning.

Skeletons in Your Closet

What constitutes a skeleton in your closet might differ greatly, depending on your circumstances. Even a conflict of interest, or appearance of conflict of interest, could be an issue if your identity were ever revealed. For many victims of sexual harassment or assault, details such as what you were wearing at the time of an incident or how long you waited to report can be unfairly held against you. If you are up against a state actor, anything that might constitute or look like illegal activity could be used against you. In the case of Thomas Drake, he had documents at his home that were made classified after he had already taken them home, making the fact that they were in his home illegal. Systematically think through and list all of these potential skeletons. If there is even the slightest possibility of them being used against you, then you must plan for them. Be aware of what your adversary might use against you. Their ethics might not be the same as yours.

Reporting Channels

In essence, exposing the truth consists of telling someone about wrongdoing. But who? How? That person or entity and the way in which they are informed can have a drastic impact on the process and outcomes for you. We will cover the most common ways of disclosing information—"reporting channels," as we will refer to them here—and talk about the advantages and disadvantages of each.

All disclosure methods can be divided into two general categories: 1) internal disclosures, where the reporting is directed to the organization that is being exposed. Examples of this would be informing a manager, boss, or someone else within an organization, or even reporting through an organization's anonymous hotline or website. The other is 2) external disclosures, where the reporting is directed to a person or entity outside of the organization being exposed. Examples of this would be reporting to a public interest organization, reporting to the press, or, for a private employee, informing a government agency.

Within these two categories we will look at a number of specific disclosure types: internal private company disclosures, internal government disclosures, external government disclosures, and disclosing to activists and public interest organizations. What method you choose can have serious ramifications for your success, so be sure to consider the advice specific to your situation, as well as consider working with a partner to help you navigate the process. We'll discuss typical partners and the advantages and disadvantages of each type of partner.

At a fundamental level, anyone who challenges the power of an organization is threatening to that organization and those within that organization. Internal reporting methods and the exposure that comes from them can lead to a reduction or removal of that power. This is threatening. A corporation's stock might fall, or a manager might be fired or even held criminally liable if systemic fraud is exposed to the public. This can lead those within the corporation to work against you. The same thing can happen within a government, where exposure of corruption can easily turn into bad publicity or forced changes to a government agency. As we all know, those in power who are threatened can fight back viciously.

There is an "inherent conflict when you're disclosing to the same institution that abused its power" says Tom Devine, legal director of the Government Accountability Project. "How can you trust that institution? It's like the same people who would be pleading guilty in court are the ones you're asking to clean up the mess whose existence they deny." Because reporting internally can pit an organization's staff against you, it is usually better to look outside an organization for an external channel. The problem is that many channels that look like external ones are actually internal channels in disguise. So it is important to make sure that any external disclosure channel that you use is independent of the organization or associated conflicts of interest, not just external to your own specific chain of command.

A human resources department is a good example of an internal channel being camouflaged as an external channel; it is purportedly there to support the company's employees, when in fact it serves to keep an organization safe and sound. This generally includes helping management tick off the required boxes to successfully fire employees. For example, when a company's inadequate response to systemic workplace harassment is made public, this can damage the reputation of an organization and lead to high legal fees and other ramifications. This spurs organizations to keep victims silent, using human resources as protection for the organization. Some estimates suggest that more than 75 percent of all workplace harassment goes unreported because victims fear retribution and termination of employment.[131]

A very public example that shows some of the dangers of internal disclosure came in the Harvey Weinstein sexual harassment scandal. At Weinstein's company, Miramax, the human resources department allegedly took no actions in response to complaints from accusers. On some occasions, it's alleged that HR forwarded the complaints about Weinstein's conduct directly to Weinstein.[132] In some instances, victims were paid off for their silence. They settled with the company and signed agreements stating that they would never disclose Weinstein's name and would even provide assistance to Miramax if legal troubles were to arise.[133] Be aware of how your disclosures might actually be routed. Internal disclosure channels can masquerade as external, and are typically not safe.

For public employees, similar internal channels are veiled as external channels. In the United States, many federal and state government agencies have Offices of the Inspector General (OIG) that are charged with investigating whistleblower claims. While structurally autonomous, these offices' primary working relationships are with managers from the same organization that you are trying to report on, so working with them should be considered carefully. OIGs have been known to be enlisted to conduct retaliatory investigations at the request of agency managers who characterize whistleblowers as criminals.

In September 2013, Dr. Katherine Mitchell, one of the first reporters in the Veteran Affairs (VA) hospital scandal in the United States, tried to confidentially file a complaint to the VA's Office of Inspector General. This was over a year and a half after she had first begun reporting internally about delays in patient care and manipulated patient wait times. Upon receiving the report, the OIG forwarded Mitchell's complaint along with her name directly to the national VA office (her boss). Instead of this disclosure quickly leading to reforms within the VA system, a month later Mitchell was put on administrative leave and subjected to an investigation by the VA. These were both clear retaliatory acts, as Mitchell has noted.[134]

It can be difficult to figure out which disclosure channel is the best to use, especially given the high potential for retaliation if you choose poorly. Be sure to do your homework and watch out for channels that are advertised as safe. They may be traps.

Internal Disclosures

The most basic form of internal disclosure is to communicate your concerns within the chain of command, such as to a supervisor or someone else in a position of power or oversight within your organization. Some companies have official reporting policies and an individual in charge, like the head of human resources or an inspector general. Some might even have an officially designated whistleblower office, as is becoming the norm in Europe. Conveying your concerns to an executive, a manager, or someone in a compliance department would also be a form of internal reporting.

Telling someone internal is generally our first instinct.[135] Most people feel a sense of duty to their own organization. They want to protect it. They want to feel that reporting an issue internally can change the organization for the better. The Government Accountability Project reports that 95 percent of whistleblowers try to disclose internally first, before turning to other methods.[136] Other researchers have put this at 84 percent for corporate whistleblowers.[137] Either way, the numbers are high, and it's clear that ethically-driven individuals often try to fix the system from the inside for the greater good. While this is admirable, the risks involved are also high, and working from within the system can easily lead to retaliation.

In 2018, the Global Business Ethics Survey found that 40 percent of the time that an employee exposed wrongs, they were retaliated against.[138] That's an incredibly high number that highlights the dangers here.

Jennifer Glover was a security guard at the Department of Energy's Nevada National Security Site when in November 2017 she was sexually assaulted by her coworkers during a training exercise. Glover used internal channels to report the assault and other sexual harassment incidents. "I followed all the appropriate protocols in reporting sexual harassment, exactly as I was trained," said Glover in a *New York Times* opinion piece. Instead of the human resources department or her supervisors taking disciplinary action against her attackers, she was retaliated against. Her security clearance was revoked and she was forced to take multiple psychological tests (which she passed). She was moved to a job in the guard shack. Finally, instead of reinstating her clearance and charging her attackers, her employer, SOC, fired Glover. Only with the public disclosure of her story in the media, and a public outcry, were politicians motivated to investigate. [139] [140] [141]

Glover's story may sound like an extreme example, but retaliation happens every day in all corners of organizations and corporations. While not all internal reporting will lead to retaliation, there are safer ways to reveal the truth. Informing someone internally, beyond what's necessary to demonstrate notice, should be avoided.

That being said, there are many circumstances where it can be beneficial to a legal case that notification of a problem has been given to the company or organization. "The trick is to provide notice in such a nonthreatening manner that it won't spark either a cover-up or retaliation," says Tom Devine. This might be asking an offhand question to your manager about an issue without any indication or hint that you are about to disclose. Consult a lawyer before attempting this.

While there are some safer methods for internal anonymous disclosure, such as anonymous hotlines and websites, and while they can offer more protections, they should still be used cautiously. By calling a hotline you are leaving a log of what number you called from and potentially leaving a recording of your voice. This is certainly not anonymous and could be linked to you. Similarly, online reporting websites should be used with reservations. Comments you submit could be linked to your identity on the basis of your style of writing or the unique information that you share.

If you are going to use one of these systems, do so only if you are using Tor or another form of online anonymization at the very least. Never use any reporting system from a work computer.

I spoke with an employee of a U.S.–based software company that has many other workers in India. This employee had used an anonymous internal method to disclose overseas fraud that the employee had discovered. By reporting the fraud, the employee saved the company millions of dollars. Unfortunately, based on the specifics of the information provided, the employee was later identified by company managers. Though the employee wasn't retaliated against, neither were they commended, thanked, or rewarded for exposing the corruption. The employee said that they would never do it again. They said that it wasn't worth it. So even if your incentives are aligned with the organization, consider reporting internally only if you can do so anonymously, with no possibility of your disclosure being linked back to your identity.

Whistleblowers and Companies: Who Benefits?

From an organizational perspective, having an individual report internally can provide a helpful early warning about wrongdoing, which could potentially cut off a scandal or a larger loss for the organization. In his book *Whistleblowers: Incentives, Disincentives, and Protection Strategies*, the lawyer and business writer Frederick D. Lipman assured readers that a "robust" whistleblower policy can "better enable the directors to detect and prevent corporate wrongdoing and major risk exposures, thereby enabling them to better perform their fiduciary duties."[142] Internal reporting is essentially framed as auditing, a system for protecting the company, but not necessarily keeping the company ethically responsible. When an employee and those in power at an organization aren't aligned in their ethics, the results of using an internal reporting channel can be disastrous.

While internal disclosure is generally not safe, basic fact-checking and gathering information internally, without tipping your hand, can be useful.

Having worked with more than seven thousand whistleblowers, Tom Devine of the Government Accountability Project has a lot of experience in this area. He identifies two advantages to raising questions to managers in a nonthreatening manner. The first is that you can do some internal fact-checking, which can confirm the accuracy of the inferences you are making from the information you have. The second is that this can remove any plausible deniability from higher-ups. If a legal case is eventually mounted, a manager can't claim "I never knew!" This was the claim from Elizabeth Holmes after her startup Theranos collapsed. Of course, she did know, because Erika Cheung, a lab associate at Theranos, had raised concerns inside the company.

By raising concerns in a non-accusatory manner, you can make sure that your disclosure will not be in vain. Using this sort of internal channel can be beneficial. Even so, you must be very careful. In some circumstances, any internal questioning should be avoided: 1) if simply asking questions would create suspicion that you are planning on disclosing information, or 2) if the information you have has such clear implications that any internal disclosure would cause immediate retaliation.

Government Disclosures

When internal disclosure appears too risky, reporting to the government is often the next option. This could take the form of going to law enforcement, to an agency that is charged with overseeing an industry, or directly to a politician or legislative committee. This disclosure channel can be internal and/or external, depending on your job. For any employee, supplier, or contractor of the government, this method would be internal, whereas it would be external for any other member of the public.

Many citizens feel that it is their government's duty to support those who attempt to expose corruption. While many governments around the world provide this support in some ways, they may actively oppose it in other ways, and governments don't always see protecting disclosers as their duty. For government employees, there may be government oversight bodies, but as with other internal channels, these might not necessarily be the best option for an individual.

Some governments have set up specific channels for members of the public to disclose information. For example, in the United States, there are specific agencies set up to receive reports on tax fraud (IRS), poor working conditions (OSHA or Department of Labor), or financial crimes and insider trading (SEC). Unfortunately, there are always cases where it is unclear which agency would be the most appropriate recipient of a disclosure.

Christopher Wylie, the whistleblower in the Cambridge Analytica scandal, worked with a journalist to reveal his information to the world. In 2018, through working with British reporter Carole

Cadwalladr, Wylie exposed CA's harvesting of user data from Facebook, harvesting which eventually played a role in Brexit and Trump's presidential campaign.[143] [144] After the story was released, the FTC began an investigation, and later Congress held a hearing to discuss Wylie's claims. Yet Wylie himself never went to the government to disclose the wrongful selling and misuse of personal data.[145] [146] It could be in this case that the unethical practices he observed were just too new for Wylie to know that there was a pathway for government investigation.

Bounty Whistleblowing

Some government disclosure pathways are set up to entice reporting, particularly in the financial sector. The Securities and Exchange Commission was created in 1934 to help restore public faith in markets following the great crash of 1929. In 2010, the Dodd-Frank Act added support for whistleblowers. This includes new monetary incentives, as well as anti-retaliation rights.[147] The Security and Exchange Commission (SEC) in the United States is an example of a generally safe reporting channel.[148] The Office of the Whistleblower within the SEC received more than 4,000 tips in 2017 and paid out over $49 million in rewards to whistleblowers for providing information. This office is set up to receive tips about corporate fraud, further aligning the interests of the whistleblower and the governmental agency. Additionally, the Supreme Court has ruled that under the act, whistleblowers are protected only if they report to the SEC, not if they report internally with management.[149]

When a government agency is aligned with the individual who is reporting crimes, particularly financial crimes, there is a better chance that things will end well for the individual. Of course, individuals should still be wary from the start, because this isn't easy. As Tom Devine told the *Financial Times*, "Corporate lawyers have a zealous campaign to have employees held criminally and civilly liable for disclosing (alleged violations) to the SEC. Every whistleblower program since 2000 has had 'anti-gag' provisions, with the dramatic exception of Dodd-Frank."[150] This won't be a simple situation where you send an email and get a check. Your employer may see you as an opportunist rather than a guardian if you take this path, but nonetheless, there are possible pathways to reap rewards for exposing the truth.

There's another issue with turning to the government: outside of specific agencies, many public employees are not equipped to work with those disclosing information. In 2002, Satyendra Kumar Dubey, a manager who was charged with overseeing the construction of a 60-kilometer highway in India, sent a letter to the Prime Minister's office exposing fraud and corruption within the project. Though Dubey clearly requested anonymity in his letter, it was forwarded with his identity to his employer. Subsequently, Dubey was shot and killed, allegedly on behalf of one of the organizations he exposed.[151] Unless a government agency has been trained in how to work with those trying to reveal information, the process can easily go awry and lead to retaliation.

Government agencies have also been known to ignore or deny disclosures demonstrating clear potential risks to public health and safety. The Nuclear Regulatory Committee (NRC) in the United States received 687 complaints from nuclear plant employees between 2010 and 2016. The NRC looked into 235 of those cases and in not one instance did it side with the individual reporting an issue.[152] Could it really be that out of 687 cases, none of them were valid? This seems quite unlikely. A 2017 report provided to the Associated Press by the nonprofit news outlet Better Government Association found that in many high-stakes cases, "NRC officials overruled staff recommendations and sided with nuclear operators in addressing the potential for plant catastrophes and potential harm to the public."

Richard Perkins, who disclosed information about NRC, told BGA, "Management tells you where they want the answer to go. If you push, you're not going to get promoted again—there are other people who are willing to say it's not a serious issue." So even if there are clear channels to report through and even if you think it's in the best interest of the agency to have these issues reported, you may still be fighting a hard uphill battle if you choose to work within the system.

In the example of the NRC, we have private employees reporting to a government agency, which is an external government reporting channel. In the OIG example, we have government employees going to a government agency, which is an internal reporting channel. These systems mimic each other because there is a similarity to the sensitivity of the information that gets reported. Both systems will look flawed if the reporting is made public. The government doesn't want to look bad in either case, whether in how they regulate the nuclear industry or in the specifics of their own intelligence secrets.

Partnering Up

"It's your one voice...and yet there now exists—that's the silver lining, a number of people and organizations that do provide this kind of support and service, including legal support, that are there and available to help you negotiate this."

—Thomas Drake, NSA whistleblower

Challenging power through disclosure is not something we typically practice over and over until we get it right. Instead, you will be heading into a gauntlet without knowing the traps and challenges that lie around every corner. Unlike a career or skill learned over time, safely disclosing information isn't typically an art that people are able to practice. Compare this to the institutions that you will be challenging, which get a chance to practice every time someone new stands up to them.

The best way to combat this lack of experience is by working with a partner—a person or group that has been through the process before and can help navigate the social, technical, and legal hurdles. You want partners with an understanding of your circumstances, an understanding of the adversaries you are up against, and an understanding of the power dynamics at play. It might be your first time going through this process, but it need not be your partner's.

Just as there are a variety of reporting channels, there are just as many types of partners. Some partners can act as a reporting channel as well—such as a journalist who can also report through their publication to the public, or an activist at an organization that can act on or release your material on behalf of the public. With these types of partners, you must be sure to consider their interests and how they compare with yours. In most cases, these types of partners are going to be beholden to their own organization's interests first. If your goals, concerns, privacy, and safety don't align with your partner's, you might want to look for a partner elsewhere.

Think through the goals you wish to achieve and your risk assessment. Use these to evaluate and rank potential partners. You need a partner that can help you achieve your goals, such as righting wrongs and notifying the public while limiting the negative consequences for you. Look for partners you can trust. Trust, above all, can be the best way to judge a partner and to create a relationship that weathers the difficult process of challenging power through information disclosure.

Even if you work with a partner such as a journalist or activist, a lawyer above all others might be the most welcome partner, too. Look for lawyers who are committed to your public interest mission and who are in sync with your objectives as someone seeking to disclose information. Lawyers can work directly on your behalf, as well as help you navigate a traditional reporting channel while maintaining alignment of their interests and yours. Engaging a lawyer can be the best way to limit negative consequences. Of course, beware that many lawyers may see a case solely as a paycheck, and could try to trade your silence for cash in a settlement. Consider their objectives and their track record carefully when evaluating a lawyer as a potential partner.

Sanitization and Partners

Deciding what to disclose to the public and what to redact is an incredibly difficult problem. You must use your own ethical code to make these decisions, or better yet, you may allow a partner to help you determine what should and should not be disclosed. Both John Doe of the Panama Papers and Edward Snowden used their journalist partners to decide what information to release and what to redact. By partnering with those who have practice and expertise in the legal, ethical, and public responsibility aspects of information release, you can have help determining what should and should not be redacted. Depending upon their expertise, partners can also help you remove any traces of your identity from the material, or can help you understand what could link you to the disclosure. Be sure to discuss this and ensure your materials can't be traced.

Which partner you reach out to depends heavily on how far along you are in the process of disclosure. Devine can't remember an instance in which someone approached GAP early on and subsequently suffered retaliation. The key is seeking help from a partner before you disclose, not after. This success is in sharp contrast to those who seek help after they are already suffering from retaliation. "When people come in at that point, it's tragic, and all we can do is minimize the damage," says Devine.

If you have already reported internally and are now being retaliated against, get a lawyer immediately. You need someone on your side who can help you navigate the ensuing legal battle, who can maximize the power of your speech, and who can lead damage control. If you are still at the point of just trying to ascertain the best way to expose the truth, start by doing your homework and by anonymously researching potential partners.

Finding the right partner to work with may take a while, but it is worth the effort. Be sure you use anonymous research techniques to figure out who might be the best fit for your circumstances. By protecting your identity as you seek help, you can limit your risks to exposure and potential retaliation.

The technical, legal, and social factors around how to safely disclose information are constantly shifting, so you need to find the most recent and relevant information. The same holds true for identifying partners to work with—you must be committed and willing to do your own research. Be sure to do it anonymously, leaving no link between you and the individuals or organizations you might end up working with.

As you consider possible partners, look for people and groups focused on the same goals as you, and who have expertise in the area where you are concerned. For example, if you are exposing bad manufacturing processes in the pharmaceutical industry, you should find a partner with experience in the industry. If you have been sexually harassed, look for a partner already active in dealing with those sorts of cases. You want someone who has been successful in supporting those who have been harassed, and who has successfully held the involved organizations, individuals, and industries accountable. By finding the right partner with experience, you can connect with those who already understand the landscape and may have context-specific resources to offer.

Investigate their previous experience working with others who decided to speak up. Have they already learned lessons by ushering others through the process before? Do they understand your circumstances? Experience is the key to success.

The best way to identify a partner is by reading. Read everything you can that is related to the topic you are disclosing: books, magazines, newspapers, blogs, the websites of nonprofit organizations. Do this all while being anonymous. Your first instinct in finding a partner might be to do a quick internet search. However, Frederik Obermaier, one of the reporters who worked with source John Doe to release the Panama Papers, exposing the Panamanian law firm Mossack Fonseca, cautions against "just Googling" for a partner. This could leave a digital trace, potentially compromising your identity later on.

Print Is Anonymous

As we outlined earlier, many systems and organizations try to track and log what you read and do on the internet. This makes websites that you visit on your daily computer or phone far from anonymous. Printed media, however, can still be acquired and read anonymously. You can go to a library relatively anonymously and read periodicals, or buy them in cash at a store. Hopefully you bought this book or borrowed it anonymously. Of course, reading physical media isn't anonymous if someone is actively watching you. Even if they are, it would be hard for them to ascertain exactly what words you are reading, especially during a day spent in a library. Along those lines, consider using a book cover on any book you might read in public as research, including this one.

When reading, be sure to think about the lens through which a journalist or potential partner sees the world. A writer's moral compass will come across in their writing. It might be important to seek out partners with whom you feel a moral affinity.

By reading articles that cover the topic you are focused on, you can find organizations, lawyers, and other potential partners working in the same area, even if you don't want to work directly with the press. Pay attention to who is being interviewed or used as references in articles. Who are the sources that are authorities in an area? Who might be aligned with your views?

In Obermaier's opinion, the key attributes to look for in a journalist are hard work and values. You don't want the ethics of an organization or an individual partner to become part of the story. You need the information you are disclosing to stand on its own. For someone challenging power, this should make sense. This viewpoint can be applied to all types of partners: in fact, you don't necessarily want a partner that is most sympathetic to your cause. Instead, you want a partner who is known for their credibility, as well as known for connecting with the public when and where it will have the most impact.

Sometimes the easiest way to find a credible partner is through an established organization that fights for the rights of those who stand up. An example would be the Government Accountability Project, which works directly with whistleblowers, and the National Women's Law Center, which launched the first U.S. legal network to combat sex discrimination faced by women and girls. Transparency International also does some case work with whistleblowers through their country advocacy and legal advice centers.

Because of their intimate knowledge of the process, advocacy organizations are a special kind of partner. They can act like a conduit, vouching for and connecting you to other partners. Most likely they already have a network of journalists, lawyers, and other public advocacy organizations right at their fingertips and they can direct you to them. Be sure to contact this type of organization anonymously. There is absolutely no reason to reveal yourself while simply doing research into potential partners. A simple one-time-use pseudonymous email address can be an effective way to reach out if the organization doesn't offer more secure methods.

Look for organizations and partners that list secure methods for communication, which could be as simple as a ProtonMail email address or a Signal phone number, or as complicated as an installation of SecureDrop (see the chapter on Partner Communication to learn more about setting up a secure ProtonMail email account). Avoid web contact forms. These are often insecure and can create a trail of data. Any partner interested in working with you should take your risks and safety seriously.

You will find that many lawyers, nonprofits, and journalists lag behind in offering secure communication channels. If a potential partner does not use secure communications, keep looking for one that does. If you must reach out to a partner that does not have a secure contact method, do your research and plan out the least risky way to approach them.

In addition to security, take some time to consider both the size of the organization and its location. There are both pros and cons to working with a large organization versus a smaller one. The main issue in working with a large organization, particularly a media organization, is that it can be hard to get their attention.

Large news organizations like the *New York Times* or the *Washington Post* might have multiple secure communication channels, but because they receive so many tips daily, it might be hard for yours to rise above the others. John Doe, the source who disclosed the Panama Papers, initially had trouble getting the media interested at all.

In their manifesto, first published on the *Süddeutsche Zeitung* website, and later in the *Panama Papers* book, Doe writes that a number of media organizations were offered the opportunity to work with them. Doe even approached WikiLeaks, but had no success.[153] Not only can it be difficult to get the attention of large organizations, it can be even more difficult to do so anonymously. So why did Doe end up working with two German journalists? It could have simply been serendipity that Doe approached a paper in Munich. Or perhaps after learning that it is hard to get the attention of large papers, Doe approached a smaller paper with two journalists who were already focused on tax evasion. Looking back, it was probably wise that Doe did not approach journalists within Panama, instead putting some literal and legal distance between them and their adversary, Mossack Fonseca.

While we won't unpack all of the various laws around the world that cover source protection and whistleblowing, it is likely that a source will be more protected in Germany than in Panama. In the 2019 World Press Freedom Index, published by Reporters Without Borders, Germany ranked 13th out of 180 countries and Panama ranked 79th.[154] So perhaps Doe realized that the location of their press partner could make them more or less secure. Be sure to consider this yourself. On the other hand, if the information you are disclosing is related to a country's national interests, going to another country could create a situation where your actions can be categorized as espionage. Maybe Doe was living in Germany, and working with a German newspaper seemed straightforward. More likely, though, Doe was methodical in researching potential partners. We may never know how Doe made these decisions, because they have successfully stayed anonymous. Be thoughtful and methodical in your choices, because they will have long-lasting implications.

Finding journalists or a partner in another country can be difficult, but there are some international organizations that can either be your partner or help you find the right one, such as the International Consortium of Investigative Journalists and Transparency International (ICIJ). Gerard Ryle, director of the ICIJ, says the organization currently receives 100 to 200 contacts a day, and sometimes those need to be connected to media partners in specific countries. "If the story isn't of huge interest to a global audience," he says, "we tend to be the conduit for a local media organization—one that we trust." Just like advocacy organizations, larger journalism organizations can act as conduits to help you find the right partner. When doing your research, try to identify organizations that might already have the right partner for you.

Family

No matter what partner you decide to work with, the process of disclosure is psychologically difficult. It will likely be "a very isolating event," says Drake. "You have to become compartmentalized. Most people don't do that very well." So check in with your family before deciding to stand up, to reveal the truth, and to take on the inevitable psychological stresses associated with that. Discuss with them, as best as you can, the burden you are taking on—but don't give them details that could potentially compromise them. Not every situation calls for keeping your family in the dark, though it can be an effective means of protecting your loved ones. Drake and Jeffrey Wigand, who exposed unethical practices in the tobacco industry and whose story was dramatized in the movie *The Insider*, both kept their families in the dark. They didn't want family members implicated in any way. Even so, the stress may have impacted Wigand's marriage.[155] If you don't find yourself in a high-stakes national-security situation, consider talking with your family and your support network. Even if you can't give them details of what you are going to do, you might be able to explain your motivations or some of what you're facing. Discuss with them the stress that you are going to be dealing with and help them understand how they can support you.

If you are in a situation where you don't feel safe or supported at home, disclosure to your family may not be a good idea. For instance, when the organizers of Líderes Campesinas started organizing women farm workers in California, they found that many were afraid to speak out about workplace abuses because of their home situations.[156] Before talking with anyone, do a risk assessment, trust your instincts, and look to confide only in those with whom you feel safe.

Lawyers

The legal landscape varies wildly around the world and from industry to industry. Partnering with a lawyer is often a necessity.

Be mindful to work with lawyers who have experience with disclosures and, if possible, who have experience with your particular industry or area of focus.

The United States and most countries around the world offer some sort of attorney-client privilege that can protect the confidentiality of your conversations.[157] This is a stronger legal protection for keeping information safe than source protection laws or "shield" laws that afford journalists protection against revealing their sources. A conversation with a lawyer will likely be safer (in legal terms) than a conversation with someone who isn't a lawyer. That said, not everyone has access to lawyers. Not all advocacy organizations will take on your case. And outside the United States, the attorney-client privilege might not exist for your particular circumstances.

"Speak to people you trust and reach out to see if there is a lawyer that would be willing to speak to you," says Chloe Caras. Caras sued Mike Isabella Concepts, the company of former *Top Chef* participant Mike Isabella, accusing Isabella and his partners of sexual harassment. In 2018 the parties settled, and afterward, MIC went bankrupt.

Caras also suggests that you should reach out to a lawyer because, she notes, they can "tell you if they don't think you have a case." Debra Katz represented Caras in her case and also represented Dr. Christine Blasey Ford, the psychology professor who accused U.S. Supreme Court Justice Brett Kavanaugh of sexual assault. Lawyers often have an upfront consultation fee, but Caras recommends "to ask if they will waive that for you—it can be costly." As with other partners, it's best to inquire about your options and get an opinion from a lawyer who has previously represented others in similar situations.

Reporting Through a Lawyer

If you are still convinced you need to disclose internally to your organization or must go to the government, consider using a lawyer as an intermediary. A lawyer can potentially keep you anonymous through the process, making sure that your disclosure is received while limiting retaliation against you.

One advantage of a lawyer, says Tom Devine, is that attorney-client privilege can potentially make your lawyer a safe place to store documentation. Evidence stored with a lawyer is harder to subpoena than if it is in your home. Of course, within the United States, attorney-client privilege does not protect conversations where the discussion or documents involve committing or furthering a crime or fraud. In the case of individuals working for the U.S. government, this scenario can be tricky because the release of classified material is a crime, and so the release of such documents is more frequently prosecuted under the Espionage Act. Therefore even in a meeting with your lawyer, if you discuss publicly releasing classified documents or committing any other crime, this could be justification for cracking your attorney-client privilege. This was the case with the FBI raid on the office of Michael Cohen, Donald Trump's former personal attorney, when the FBI must have considered that the communications and materials in Cohen's office related to the furtherance of a crime.[158]

A lawyer's goals might not always be the same as your goals. A lawyer is positioned to uphold the law while making sure that your legal rights are protected. But this can sometimes be at odds with your ethical motivations. Ben Wizner, director of the ACLU's Speech, Privacy, and Technology Project, suggests that if Snowden had come to him first, he might have told Snowden not to disclose any information, since the disclosure would be illegal. On the other hand, Wizner has been working with Snowden for years since he fled to Russia, helping him minimize his liability and risk. It's important to find a lawyer who understands the intricacies of your situation and who aligns with your ethics. Consider how you frame your situation to legal partners: you may get different advice depending on how you ask your question.

When contacting lawyers, be wary of websites that are outdated and have weak security features. Many lawyers still rely on insecure website contact forms, unencrypted email, and basic telephones for initial contact. If you can find a lawyer on Wire, Signal, or another secure messenger service, use that channel first. Lack of secure communication can make it easier for an adversary to surveil or identify you when contacting a lawyer. Furthermore, if a lawyer doesn't have a secure method of communication, it could show that they might not be considering your digital security. Lawyers have in some cases relied on attorney-client privilege as an excuse for not being up to speed on privacy-focused digital messaging systems. You might consider face-to-face meetings with a lawyer, limiting any digital trail. This might be the most secure way to initiate contact.

Some lawyers are certainly up to using security best practices and have established new ways of collaborating with the press. Jesselyn Radack, who heads WHISPeR at ExposeFacts, has supported and represented a number of high-profile intelligence community individuals, including Thomas Drake, John Kiriakou, and Edward Snowden. She suggests that some lawyers know and trust certain journalists with whom they work. By having the lawyer attend the meeting of the journalist and source, it is possible to "wrap it within attorney client privilege," provided that discussing the information isn't illegal in the first place.

The Media

Public opinion is often the key factor in turning the tide against corrupt institutions as seen with the Pentagon Papers, the #MeToo movement, revelations of the tobacco industry's addictive practices, reports of Pfizer's illegal antibiotic trials on Nigerian children (and alleged blackmail of Nigerian officials), revelations of torture and prisoner abuse by American soldiers at Abu Ghraib prison in Iraq, coverage of the Catholic Church's sex abuse scandal, Edward Snowden's NSA revelations, and many other cases. By working with the press, you can help the public become informed and engaged. Once exposed, it is only a matter of time before a government, an organization, or a corporation must respond and then hopefully change for the better.

In the U.S., under the Whistleblower Protection Act, disclosing information is legally protected, except in the following scenarios: 1) the information is classified, 2) its release would be prohibited by a statute, or 3) releasing the information would be in violation of an agreement you've signed. That was reaffirmed by the Supreme Court in *Department of Homeland Security v. MacLean*. But it's not as simple as that, because going to the press puts you in the crosshairs of a government or corporation, especially in many places outside of the U.S. So be mindful of the situation you are walking into from the very beginning.

In some contexts, the system for legal disclosure is so broken that individuals must turn to the press. Edward Snowden, for example, knew that as a contractor for an intelligence agency he had almost no protections for reporting internally to the government. He now says that there should be major reforms for whistleblowing laws. As he told *The Guardian* in 2016, "The sad reality of today's policies is that going to the inspector general with evidence of truly serious wrongdoing is often a mistake. Going to the press involves serious risks, but at least you've got a chance."[159]

Before you contact a reporter, consider how you would like your disclosure to play out. Be strategic in your communication. Above all else, when working with the press, make sure the story starts with the issues that you are exposing, and not you. Too many times, particularly in sexual harassment situations, the story can end up focused on you instead of the perpetrator. Making the story personal can in some cases help to get the public on your side, but be careful what you reveal at first. Once your identity gets connected to a story on the basis of information that you provide, you can be subject to various types of retaliation. Your role in the story may be important, and the story may ultimately not be one you're able to tell without revealing your part in it. But remember your goals. The real story is the truth you are revealing. Make sure your partner from the press understands this. If you are the victim, think carefully about how you frame your story, and consider getting a lawyer before approaching the press. That might be the best way to make sure you remain protected.

Just as with any partner, you must be sure you are working with someone who understands the intricacies of the topic you are exposing. Journalism inherently involves research, and someone with an in-depth understanding can more quickly ascertain the value of the information you have and confirm its validity.

FOIA Requests

In some circumstances it's possible to tip off journalists about documents that exist without actually providing the documents. This allows journalists to attempt to access the information using other means, such as a Freedom of Information Act request. Unfortunately, sometimes when FOIA requests for documents are very specific, it can be a tip-off that someone internal has disclosed information. This seems to have been the case with Terry Albury, a former FBI agent who pleaded guilty to leaking documents to *The Intercept*. Albury had sent a number of documents to *The Intercept*, which subsequently made FOIA requests for some of those documents. The documents that were published on *The Intercept*'s website showed a date that was different than the FOIA-requested dates, leading the FBI to believe that the document was leaked from someone inside the FBI rather than coming from a FOIA request. Furthermore, similar to the Reality Winner situation, investigators saw that Albury had looked at these documents on his work computer, tying him to the leaks. It might have been better for Albury never to have opened the documents on his computer, but instead to have simply described them to a journalist.[160] [161]

If you find the right partner, they can also act as a filter for the public. Rather than deciding yourself what is appropriate to release, you can allow a media partner to make that decision. This can help make it clear that your motivation is to help the public, not yourself. This was the case with Snowden, who asked that *The Guardian* and other media outlets decide what information should be released and what should be redacted. The media partners had to weigh what might harm intelligence operations against making sure that enough information was released, so that the public could make their own decisions about whether the NSA surveillance programs were ethical and in the public interest.[162]

Beyond having an understanding of the topic, a journalist partner should be able to convey the issues involved to the public. Edward Snowden was very deliberate in approaching Glenn Greenwald. He thought Greenwald would be the best at conveying information to the public. While Greenwald may not have been as up to speed as others on some of the underpinnings of the technology that Snowden was revealing, his ability to convey the arguments mattered more for Snowden.

Compared to lawyers, these journalist partners offer both advantages and disadvantages. When considering what information to release, reporters tend to be more willing to work at the boundaries of what is legal. The press can publish and release documents that they consider to be in the public interest, but few lawyers would be willing to do this. However, by comparison, the ability of a journalist to keep a source anonymous and conversations confidential is weak.

Journalists and publishers have long seen value in citing and protecting anonymous sources when that's the best way to get information to the public, but courts around the world have not always upheld this point of view. Accordingly, most media organizations will closely scrutinize any use of anonymous sourcing, with the goal of avoiding it whenever possible in favor of sources or information that can be made public. Margaret Sullivan, the former public editor of the *New York Times*, says that when "journalists agree to anonymity, it should be for an important purpose," not just to make a story work or because "we like somebody's clever-sounding quote."

From a journalist's point of view, they will want assurances that the information they are getting is correct, as well as assurance that they're not being used by a would-be source. In many cases, they will want to do this by learning your identity. Unfortunately, this is at odds with your best protection as a source, being anonymous. You will have to work with your partner to figure out what suits both of you the best and strike the right balance between protecting yourself and having maximal impact. Moreover, even in the U.S., where press freedoms are relatively high, there is no guarantee that a reporter faced with jail time won't reveal your identity. This is a reason that it might be to the journalist's benefit as well as yours for you to remain anonymous.

Unlike attorney-client privilege, confidentiality between a reporter and a source is protected by relatively weak laws around the world. Before approaching a journalist, research the legal context and relative press freedoms in a given country. Generally speaking, press freedoms are stronger in North America and Western Europe, but depending on what you are exposing, you might choose to work outside of those contexts.[163] Check https://rsf.org/en/ranking for more details on press freedoms around the world.

Reporters' jobs and reputations depend on their ability to protect conversations with sources. Many journalists have been at the forefront of using and championing secure communication technology. By working with a journalist who has already been using these technologies, you can increase your chances of staying private and/or anonymous.

Intelligence Reporters

Journalists who have worked with high-profile sources in the intelligence community will have practice securing conversations and the identities of sources. They will also have their own rules about how they work with sources, perhaps asking to meet only in person or avoiding conversations via phone. Working with these types of journalists can be a benefit, because they will likely have well-tested procedures. On the other hand, intelligence reporters might be tracked more than others, and working with them could potentially make you a target. As with any potential partner, you should evaluate the risks and benefits of an alliance with any particular investigative reporter.

Media organizations on the whole have been pushing the boundaries of how to work with sources more securely. Recently many news organizations have published tips pages that list the methods for a source to provide information. *The Intercept*'s tips page even suggests that sources might want to first consult an attorney: "Before deciding to bring your story to a journalist, you might want to consult an attorney to better understand your options and risks."[164]

When deciding upon potential partners, consider how invested an organization is in protecting sources. Media organizations that have spent resources to implement and maintain anonymous tip systems might be better candidates. A great place to start is the directory of media organizations with SecureDrop installations verified by the Freedom of the Press Foundation.[165]

Despite the inherent competition among media organizations, collaboration is on the rise. In 2010, WikiLeaks collaborated with *El País, Der Spiegel, Le Monde, The Guardian,* and the *New York Times* to redact and release 220 of the U.S. diplomatic cables given to WikiLeaks by Chelsea Manning.[166] [167] In 2016, the International Consortium of Investigative Journalists and *Süddeutsche Zeitung* brought together over a hundred media partners to investigate the Panama Papers. More than 300 journalists worked together to sift through the 11.5 million documents. It would have been impossible for any one media organization to do the necessary research to tell this story, and without these types of partnerships, the source John Doe would have had minimal impact.

As someone attempting to disclose information, you should have one primary contact, but there might be occasions when it is good for your contact to pull in other partners. Journalists might have lawyers or other contacts that would be good for you to speak with anonymously before a story is released.

You should not be counting on a journalist for legal advice or even advice on how to be safe. "Journalists are a best judge of what is good journalism—they're not the best judges of what is a good lawsuit," says Sharon Weinberger, D.C. bureau chief at Yahoo! News and a former editor at *Foreign Policy* and *The Intercept*. Consider carefully who you should contact for certain advice. It all depends on the context and their background.

Self-Publishing

In the last decade, some have found success by releasing information on the internet themselves, particularly on social media. Some have used the internet anonymously to publish and disseminate information themselves on various publishing platforms. Consider the risks of this first and foremost, particularly with regard to your identity, before you publish on your own.

Many of the #MeToo movement revelations of sexual harassment and assault have been self-published, with a number of women—some powerful, some previously unknown—bravely taking public ownership of their own traumatic stories online. Actresses Kate Upton and Ariane Bellamar spoke out publicly on Twitter about their sexual harassment by powerful men. This in turn opened up a conversation that led others to come forward.[168] [169] Aside from Twitter, the blogging platform Medium has been chosen by many to tell their stories. Novelist and children's writer Anne Ursu even used Medium to publish the results of a survey about sexual harassment in children's book publishing, shining a light on industry-wide issues.[170]

A cascade of revelations have been published on social media, and with each one, others have been inspired to tell their stories. In many cases, prominent women opted to self-publish revelations, allowing them, not their alleged harassers or the media, to control the story. But for people who are not famous or prominent, it can be hard to speak up in this way and get positive results. Many would be retaliated against.

There are exceptional cases. Self-publishing on social media has in some cases opened up conversations between the accuser and accused. When former *Community* showrunner Dan Harmon alluded to bad behavior on his part in a January 1, 2018 tweet, Megan Ganz, a former writer for the show, responded: "Care to be more specific? Redemption follows allocution." A public conversation ensued between the two on Twitter, in which Ganz detailed how she was affected: "It took me years to believe in my talents again, to trust a boss when he complimented me and not cringe when he asked for my number. I was afraid to be enthusiastic, knowing it might be turned against me later." This conversation eventually led Harmon to publicly apologize, detailing his sexual harassment of Ganz and seeking to make amends for his behavior.[171] Again, this is an exceptional case, and taking this approach could instead lead to retaliation: job loss, loss of reputation in an industry, and even charges of libel or slander.

Others have used speaking directly to the public through online video to capture attention and gain support. After years of frustration when no one listened to his concerns, Michael DeKort, an engineer who worked on equipment used in U.S. Coast Guard boats at Lockheed Martin, posted a video on YouTube. In the ten-minute video, DeKort sits at his desk and reads a prepared speech explaining the issues.[172] A few months after posting, DeKort was fired from Lockheed Martin. Finally, in 2010, after years of court battles, DeKort's whistleblower case was settled with Lockheed Martin for an undisclosed amount. This story may have ended well, but consider the years of legal battles that DeKort had to withstand, all while out of work.[173] If DeKort had gone to a partner, particularly a lawyer, instead of self-publishing, he might not have had to deal with such serious repercussions for trying to do the right thing.

While the strategy of self-publishing has achieved some success, particularly when a prominent name has lent validity to a claim, publicly linking your identity to your accusations will not help protect you against retaliation. Using your own name should be viewed as a last resort. Instead, work with a partner, or, if no one will support you, self-publish anonymously.

One of the biggest issues with anonymous self-publishing is that you may inadvertently include a piece of information that links back to your identity, leaving you open to retaliation. Without a partner, you are solely responsible for the sanitization of your information and the anonymization of your connection to a publishing platform. Even those who practice anonymization daily can slip up from time to time, and when they do, their identities can be revealed and their anonymity lost. Even worse, if you create enemies online or become the target of a collective like 4chan, it's highly likely that your identity will be revealed. So be cautious in self-publishing, because your identity will likely be implicated immediately. You need to be ready for this. It's far safer to work with a partner in order to plan out a solid strategy.

Doxing

For those who might not be aware, identifying people who attempt to be anonymous online or even revealing personal information about someone has become a technique used on the internet to attack individuals. The term "doxing" is a relatively new word that comes from "documents" or "docs," and this method was originally used by hackers in the 1990s to attack other hackers. Removing someone's anonymity was one of the only ways that hackers could attack another. [174] More recently, however, doxing has become popular with groups like 4chan and others who seek to retaliate publicly against an individual or group.

In doxing, personal information is compiled and released openly on the internet. Pastebin.com is a typical anonymous posting site where information is released publicly.

As someone attempting to release information, be careful about who you are naming and consider the retaliation methods that they may use. Particularly, consider the damaging consequences for yourself or others through public disclosure of your identity and the information that you have. Keep this in mind when doing a risk assessment, and consider carefully any skeletons that you might have in your closet that could be discovered and revealed through a dox.

Internal Partners

Talking about disclosing information internally at your company or organization is dangerous. The organization should be thought of as your adversary, not your partner. Be very careful about deciding who to trust, especially within your organization. Once you tell someone internally, your anonymity and the protection that comes with it have the potential to be lost forever. Instead, as we've described here, look for partners external to your organization.

There are some internal actions that you can take that may prove beneficial. Depending on your circumstances, you may want to have careful, nonthreatening conversations to gather more information or confirm your suspicions. You may want to talk to trusted colleagues to gain internal support, or even to responsibly provide notice about an issue internally. If you are employed by a U.S. government agency, reporting to an Inspector General's office would be a good example of the last approach. Under these circumstances, your communications with the Inspector General should be protected by law.

Don't be tempted to consider the Inspector General your partner. You should always keep in mind that internal partners may have internal pressures that will make them compromise your goals. Until you're able to establish complete trust, keep an internal partner at arm's length, because you don't know if they might waver in their support of you. Their first duty is generally to the government or organization that pays their salary.

The same can be said for reporting to human resources or a compliance department. Officers in these departments are *not* a true partner. You need to think of them more as your adversary.

If you must report to and work with someone internally, be sure you also have an outside partner. In particular, a lawyer can be a great outside partner in this context. Their interests are aligned with yours as part of their job.

Coworkers are the only internal partner that you don't need to consider your adversary right from the beginning. They may not be a partner in the sense that we've described so far, but trusted coworkers can be important with respect to checking and supporting your claims. If you are going to risk discussing wrongdoing with a coworker, however, be sure to do it in a way that doesn't single you out as someone who intends to challenge the power of the organization. You don't want to tip your hand, but you do want to be able to verify the claims you are about to make. Try to verify information with coworkers without exposing yourself.

The other reason to work with coworkers is to create a support network for when you do expose the truth. When everything is made public, you will want your coworkers to support you and not to turn against you. The more support you have after disclosing, the higher your chances of success. Be sure to surround yourself with a network of coworkers who you know will have your back.

Public Interest and Activist Organizations

Sometimes the safest external channel is reporting to an organization that has been working on behalf of the public for a long time. Whether you are exposing issues around health, the environment, food and drug safety, sexual harassment, or even bad manufacturing practices, there are likely organizations that are already actively working on changing the industry, culture, or government in these areas. Organizations that do this work on behalf of the public are known as public interest organizations.

Their cousins, activist organizations and even individual activists, are often focused on issues that affect only a subset of the public or have a specific goal in mind, such as the ethical treatment of animals. Both of these types of partners will have unique perspectives, intentions, and missions. In some cases they might not be in sync with your goals, which can be a problem. Be sure to seek out partners whose perspective, ethics, and goals align with yours.

Additionally, be sure to seek out those with experience working with people who want to disclose information. The story of Matt Diaz is an unfortunate example of what can go wrong. In 2005, Diaz, a JAG Corps officer at Guantanamo Bay detention facility, sent an anonymous greeting card to the Center for Constitutional Rights. Inside was a list of names of detainees at Guantanamo. At that point in time, the U.S. government had no plans to release this information, and had not released any information about the individuals being held. Without their names, legal representation for the detainees could not be arranged, leaving detainees bereft of any legal support.

Unfortunately, when the anonymous envelope reached the center, there was no way to get in touch with the sender. Without knowing best practices for working with someone trying to anonymously disclose information, the center (advised by its lawyers) told the court about the material it had received. The court ordered the center to turn over the materials, and shortly thereafter the FBI became involved. A military trial ensued, and eventually

Diaz was sentenced to six months in prison and dismissed from the military with a dishonorable discharge.

At the same time, the Guantanamo facility changed its position, and the names of the detainees were released under the Freedom of Information Act.[175] [176] This book is filled with examples of courageous individuals being retaliated against, only to have laws change after their disclosure.

There are two big takeaways from the Diaz story: 1) be sure to pick a partner that has experience working with information disclosure and 2) establishing ongoing communication and a relationship of trust with a partner can potentially protect your identity more than simply dropping off information anonymously. Diaz and the Center for Constitutional Rights were aligned in their goals, yet that was not enough to protect Diaz. The Center and Diaz both lacked knowledge of best practices for how to disclose information safely.

If there isn't a public interest organization that fits well with the information that you are trying to expose, it's likely you might be able to find an activist or activist organization that will work with you. Sometimes the information being exposed doesn't fit with an internal, government, or even public interest organization channel. In this instance, working with an organization or individual that has a focused mission that is aligned with the information that you have and is aligned with your intentions might be the best option.

Public interest organizations and their activist counterparts can be more than just reporting channels. They can also be a partner to you. Before partnering with any organization, however, it's important to understand their political positioning and the public's perception of these groups before approaching them. The way a given organization is viewed by the public can shift dramatically over time.

As someone ready to challenge power, you need to understand the motivations, pros, and cons of those channels that you are considering, especially activist organizations. Be sure to do your own research before choosing a path. Some activist organizations work on behalf of the public at large, whereas others focus on advocating for specific groups. The issues that groups focus on will vary as well, with organizations such as the ACLU and the NAACP in the U.S. addressing a broad range of issues, and others, such as Compassion Over Killing, focusing specifically on an issue such as ending animal abuse.

Of all the organizations out there fighting for change in your area of interest, look for those with a history of successfully implementing change. These are the organizations that will have the resources and contextual knowledge to guide you. Even better, look for organizations that have previously worked with individuals successfully; they will have learned specific lessons that you can build upon to support your work.

Working with an activist organization can potentially be a great way to make lasting change. These organizations have intimate knowledge of the political landscape and how to navigate it. Having been focused on a topic for a long time, an activist organization will know the key players and their motivations. Be careful, though: an organization might not have your best interests in mind. Their goal of making change happen might supersede protecting you.

Depending on an organization's size, they may have a legal department to help you navigate the legal landscape, or they may have a law firm that they've worked with before. Of course, this legal advice will come from the perspective of the organization, protecting them first and foremost, not you. One way to protect yourself is by establishing a separate retainer that specifies that the attorney's primary duty is to you, not the organization. Additionally, these organizations might not be prepared to work with individuals anonymously. They likely won't be experienced with digital security best practices the way a journalist may be. So take your time in deciding how to safely work together. Exceptions to this would be working with organizations that are advocates for digital rights, such as the Electronic Frontier Foundation, or that have a specific history of working with anonymous individuals.

Whistleblower organizations, on the other hand, are a subset of organizations that are focused on working with and supporting individuals who are ready to disclose information. These organizations fight for whistleblower rights, but can also guide you through the process. Depending on the industry and information you have, one of these organizations might be a good fit or at least a good starting point for a referral.

A number of organizations are also focused on supporting sexual harassment victims and those who stand up for equality in the workplace. These organizations and their whistleblower-focused cousins bring together legal, journalistic, and advocacy resources under one roof, creating a safe place to start when looking for help. They will usually have lawyers on staff who know the legal landscape and likely have trusted journalists that they've worked with in the past. In some cases, the organizations can act as their own publisher, breaking stories on their own. They may be able to pull together a team from other organizations, such as outside lawyers, journalists, and activist organizations, to set up a multipronged approach to exposing the truth and informing the public.

Check the appendix for listings of organizations to reach out to when trying to stand up and reveal the truth. They are ready to help you, but it's up to you to safely contact them.

Partner Communication

"I think from the perspective of a source, if you've got something to say and it's important, I think it's far better to develop a trusting relationship . . . over a period of time with a reporter than to try to drop something anonymously, because the chances of a fuck-up or not understanding or a miscue . . . can be pretty high if you're not really thinking about this with another person in advance."

—John Cook, Investigations Editor, Business Insider

The best way to expose the truth is by building a relationship and establishing trust with a partner—enabling you to work together to challenge power and to support each other through the process. Think of this as a relationship rather than a transaction, one that you should invest in. By the time you are ready to hand over information to a partner, you will feel comfortable with how it will be handled.

Many first timers try to anonymously deliver a piece of information to a partner like in an old spy novel or movie: by simply leaving a folder and walking away. This method has worked for some, but usually it fails miserably, with the source losing their job, being publicly identified, or in a number of cases going to jail. I do not recommend this method. Too much can go wrong.

The biggest issue with trying to just drop something off is actually doing it anonymously.

First of all, you must be 100 percent positive that you haven't left traces of yourself behind in the materials that you are delivering. In this era of 24-hour security cameras and digital tracking, it is nearly impossible. Outside of spy novels and movies, this only works if you have a high degree of technical expertise and practice in data gathering, sanitization, and anonymity methods.

Speaking about Matt Diaz, who was sentenced to six months in prison, disbarred, and dishonorably discharged for sending a list of Guantanamo detainees to the Center for Constitutional Rights,[177] Danielle Brian, executive director of the Project on Government Oversight, points out that the anonymous drop-off method is highly problematic: "Even people who are obviously good guys...if they aren't sort of trained in how to protect source, this is the kind of terrible thing that could happen."

If the recipient of the information isn't familiar with best practices for sanitizing information or protecting identities, or perhaps doesn't know how to use the information responsibly, things will go wrong.

A partner might want to protect you, but they might not know the best way to do it. You must protect yourself first and foremost.

Examples of the anonymous drop-off method working well are the two releases of portions of Donald Trump's 1995 and 2005 federal tax returns. In both instances, individuals with access to these documents used postal mail to send copies to Susanne Craig at the *New York Times* and to David Cay Johnston, an independent journalist, both of whom published the documents online. If any identifiers had been discernible on these documents, the individual that sent them could have been found. In the same regard, if there had been handwriting on the envelope, or the documents had been sent and postmarked from locations less generic than large cities in New York, the senders could potentially have been identified.

In the anonymous drop-off method, the source becomes solely responsible for the sanitization of any information provided, though this doesn't mean that the partner is removed from responsibility. In the previous example, the *New York Times* chose not to publish photos of the package itself, which likely helped the source remain anonymous. Johnston, on the other hand, scanned and posted photos of the envelope that the document was sent in (likely to prove the document's veracity), which did have the potential to identify the sender. This divergence in practice should make it clear that without prior communication with a partner, the source cannot control how the information will be used or released. One can only hope that the recipient of the information will make safe decisions to protect your identity.

In the case of Reality Winner and the anonymous mailing of a classified document to *The Intercept*, the delivery turned out not to be anonymous. Information linking Winner was discovered in the document itself, and the postmark of Augusta, Georgia, made it easy for investigators to narrow in on her. Regardless of whether you agree with Winner's ethics, her information sanitization process was not strong enough to remove the bread crumbs that compromised her identity.

The other issue with this method is that it can totally confound the person on the receiving end. You may believe the information you have tells a specific story, but more than likely you will have failed to provide your recipient with the necessary context. Did you forget a key piece of information? Did you include an overview or summary of its significance?

The International Consortium of Investigative Journalists (ICIJ) receives hundreds of tips a day. A lot of the tips don't have enough context to make them actionable. "Someone yesterday emailed me through a chain of emails, basically a spreadsheet of names and numbers," says Gerard Ryle, director of the ICIJ. "It means nothing to me without having a chance to talk to the source." Without this specific context or a way to talk with the source, the recipient is likely unable to act on or even decipher what you have provided.

So don't just drop off information and hope for the best. It might feel like the easiest and safest way, but it's probably the least responsible to you and the impact you hope to have. More than likely, you will just point the finger at yourself, ruining your chance of changing things for the better and potentially putting yourself in jail.

Instead, build a relationship with a partner that has been through the process before. By leaning on their history and knowledge, you can be safer in challenging power.

So how do you start a relationship? The first step is obviously reaching out and contacting someone, but you must do it in a safe way, one that doesn't compromise your identity and can serve as a handshake.

Reaching Out

By this point you should be comfortable using an anonymous mindset of compartmentalization to consider your actions and conduct anonymous research. These techniques will be required before you reach out to a partner. You should also already have done research into who would be a good partner to contact.

In your first contact message to a potential partner, your priorities should be: 1) establishing a safe mode of communication, 2) getting your partner excited to work with you, and 3) learning enough so that you can decide if they can be trusted. The first point is the most important: without a safe way to communicate, you won't be able to move forward.

When reaching out, you should always do so anonymously—or more specifically pseudonymously. By using an alias you can make it more difficult for the person with whom you are communicating (and anybody watching) to discover your true identity. Use the safest methods available when doing so. For example, contacting a lawyer through a secure instant messenger would be better than calling them or using a web contact form. Make sure you do so using a newly created pseudonymous account, compartmentalizing the initial contact from your true identity or any other accounts you might have. This way you can be sure that any initial communication can't be traced back to you.

Harassment and Lawyers

If you have been or are being harassed or abused, anonymity might not be your first thought. Consider who might be looking at your call log or emails. You may think in this case that anonymity doesn't matter, or that perhaps you'll eventually have to forgo anonymity anyway if you want to report your harassment. But anonymity can also offer secure communications without leaving a trace. If you have any inkling that someone might retaliate against you if they know you are reaching out to a lawyer or other partner, be careful in how you contact potential partners. Using a burner phone or emailing from a throwaway account can be great options. You can also tell your partner to never call you or reach out to you, limiting chances that someone else could see an incoming message from them. Be careful and thoughtful, especially if you're in a situation where you believe your communications could be scrutinized and put you in harm's way.

Many times, though, a partner will not have a secure way of contacting them listed publicly, or they might not be aware of the best applications or techniques for safe communication. Instead you will have to reach out to them pseudonymously through a less safe method and then work with them to establish a secure communication channel.

An example of this might be getting on Tor and creating a new pseudonymous email address to reach out to a partner. This way, you can create an email address that is in no way associated with your true identity (your computer, internet connection, and even your writing style).

Edward Snowden, the NSA contractor who released classified documents in 2013, used this technique when trying to establish contact with Laura Poitras, a documentary filmmaker who had previous experience with encryption. Snowden didn't have Poitras' contact information, so he sent an anonymous email to Micah Lee at the Electronic Frontier Foundation, asking for her email address. The fact that he started by contacting someone at the EFF, even anonymously, made it clear to Poitras and Lee that his message should be taken seriously. In his first email to Poitras, Snowden prioritized discussing a safer way to communicate. You must first of all be clear and upfront about your safety, which will set the standard for all of your future communications with a partner.

Laura,

At this stage I can offer nothing more than my word. I am a senior government employee in the intelligence community. I hope you understand that contacting you is extremely high risk and you are willing to agree to the following precautions before I share more. This will not be a waste of your time.

The following sounds complex, but should only take minutes to complete for someone technical. I would like to confirm out of email that the keys we exchanged were not intercepted and replaced by your surveillants. Please confirm that no one has ever had a copy of your private key and that it uses a strong passphrase. Assume your adversary is capable of one trillion guesses per second. If the device you store the private key and enter your passphrase on has been hacked, it is trivial to decrypt our communications.

Understand that the above steps are not bullet proof, and are intended only to give us breathing room. In the end if you publish the source material, I will likely be immediately implicated. This must not deter you from releasing the information I will provide.

Thank you, and be careful.

Citizen Four [178]

This email is a good example of what you should do. Snowden, a.k.a. Citizen Four, asked to shift to a more secure mode of communication, prioritizing his safety first and foremost. He gave Poitras opportunities to show that she could be trusted by taking his requests seriously. By conveying that he held a position in the government and had a high level of technical understanding, Snowden provided incentives to his potential partner to take him seriously and contact him back.

Laura Poitras and Edward Snowden continued their conversations. Over time they learned to trust each other, building a relationship through which they revealed countless truths about how the American government was actively collecting data on U.S. citizens.[179]

After the initial contact, your focus needs to be on building a working relationship with your partner. Though the process may sound strange, a relationship with a partner that is built on mutual respect, like a marriage, will go much further in supporting your goals.

"In my experience, the best way to decrease your risks of being identified is actually to have a relationship with the reporter and develop a relationship of trust," says John Cook, investigations editor at Business Insider and former editor-in-chief of *The Intercept*. "One in which you can talk openly about how you're going to communicate and how you're gonna keep from creating a record that could later be discovered."

First and foremost, you and your partner should discuss and agree on ways of working together. This can remove the full weight of the process from your shoulders. Instead, you can share the burden with your partner.

Establishing Trust

Once you have reached out and established a method of communicating with a partner, you will need to work together to figure out the rest of the process. The key to this will be establishing trust, even if your identity is pseudonymous. Just as in any relationship, you need to know that the person you are working with will respect your needs.

"The relationship of trust is a more tricky one when your source may be someone you'll never meet," says Margaret Sullivan. As the public editor of the *New York Times*, Sullivan pushed to use named sources, but still believes that in some circumstances anonymous sources are required. "There has to be a careful negotiation and a careful dance that goes on between the source and the reporter—inching toward some kind of agreement about what I'm going to give you and how you're going to use it and how you'll identify me and how you'll protect me."

As Sullivan notes, asking questions, discussing the process, and establishing commitments is key. This is potentially your livelihood on the line. Make sure you feel comfortable with your partner before you start sharing everything. It will take time to build trust. Be patient, ask questions, and be sure to set and meet commitments.

Above all else, setting expectations and meeting them will go a long way toward forming a trustful working relationship with your partner. Do what you say you are going to do. If you say you will call tomorrow night at 8 p.m., do it on the dot. By meeting commitments, you and your partner will form a relationship where you can lean on each other, knowing that you have each other's backs.

Gabriel Dance, Deputy Investigations Editor at the *New York Times*, notes that responsibilities go both ways: "We take it very seriously to protect [sources] and their personal information." It isn't simply the partner's job to meet the expectations of the tipster, he says, "it's up to you as well to stick to your word and bring a level of responsibility to this relationship."

Perhaps the best way to establish trust with a partner is asking questions of each other and thinking through the process of exposing information together. Here are some reasonable questions to use as a starting point:

- As my partner, how will you protect me, especially considering my specific adversaries?
- How will you protect the information I provide?
- Are there safer ways we could communicate?
- How will we verify each other, so that our communications aren't compromised?
- What is our schedule for communicating?
- What are ways this information could identify me?
- How will you verify my claims without identifying me?
- What is our timeline?
- Are there other partners I should talk with? A lawyer? A journalist?
- What are our backup plans in case our communication or my identity is compromised?
- Who else at your organization or otherwise will know about our conversations? Can we limit who knows?

The Panama Papers include a good example of a strong relationship of trust formed by the source John Doe (the pseudonym they gave themselves) and the journalists Bastian Obermayer and Frederik Obermaier at *Süddeutsche Zeitung*. The three worked together for over a year. At the time of the release, the Panama Papers constituted the "biggest leak in the history of data journalism" according to Edward Snowden, with over 11.5 million documents provided to the journalists.[180] This type of long-term safe communication and large delivery of information, all while maintaining anonymity, was only possible because of a strong relationship of trust. Note that at the time of writing, John Doe's true identity is still not known.[181]

The relationship started first with a simple anonymous opening to Bastian Obermayer via a messaging app: "Hello. This is John Doe. Interested in data?" The message caught Obermayer's attention, likely because it went directly to him, not to a general intake box at an organization. According to Doe's manifesto, they had previously submitted a tip on WikiLeaks' online tip system and had contacted other "prominent and capable media organizations," but none responded. So instead Doe went directly to a journalist.

When Obermayer asked how they would get the data, Doe provided a focused response:

I would like to assist but there are a couple of conditions. You need to understand how dangerous and sensitive some of this information is. My life is in danger, if my identity is revealed. I've spent the past several weeks considering how to handle this. We will only chat over encrypted channels. No meeting, ever. The choice of stories is obviously up to you.

In this message Doe makes it clear the importance of the information and how it is connected to their livelihood. Doe sets a standard for communication—encrypted only. This also provides a clue that Doe had done enough anonymous research to make safe communication the priority. By saying this upfront, Doe made it clear that to establish trust, there must be a focus on protecting communications and their anonymity.

After the initial contact with Doe, Obermayer brought in the journalistic partner Frederik Obermaier to work alongside him. Though having two partners to work with instead of one may sound complicated, it worked well in this situation, likely due to the fact that Obermaier and Obermayer already had a strong and trusting relationship.

John Doe is likely most public and prolific whistleblower in recent years who has been able to maintain anonymity over a long period of time and accomplish so much by working with journalists. There are a number of factors that contribute to this success, but the most important is likely that the journalists that Doe chose to work with have never known Doe's true identity. By having this at the core of their relationship, Doe and the journalists were protected. The other factor is that Doe and the journalists focused on encrypted communication systems to help prolong the pseudonymous relationship.

Last, while this is conjecture, it could be that Doe's identity was protected because his adversaries didn't have enough power to find him. Remember this wasn't a state actor that Doe was aligned against, but a law firm in Panama. Of course, when the documents were revealed, many powerful politicians around the world were implicated. If Doe's adversary had the backing of a state actor, perhaps it would have been harder to maintain a long-term relationship with journalists, but we can't be sure. Nonetheless, the way Obermayer, Obermaier, and Doe worked together is emblematic of a successful collaboration.

Verification

Another factor in all communication, and especially important when trying to maintain pseudonymity, is verifying that the person on the other end of the line is who they say they are. This doesn't necessarily mean knowing their actual identity, but rather being able to verify that each conversation contains the same person as the last conversation. You should be mindful of this from the very beginning, especially during the process of reaching out.

In the case of Snowden, where his adversary was the NSA, he was well aware of these issues, notably the need to verify that the digital Poitras was the real Poitras. He came up with a novel solution to this problem. Snowden requested that Micah Lee, who knew Poitras and who worked at the Electronic Frontier Foundation, publicly tweet Poitras' public encryption key, "1EBF 5F15 850C 540B 3142 F158 4BDD 496D 4C6C 5F25." By doing so, Snowden was able to verify Poitras through the trusted digital identity of Lee. Even if the NSA compromised Poitras' accounts, they would also have to compromise Lee's Twitter account in order to trap Snowden.

The problem of verifying that accounts are actually controlled by the people you want them to be has been around for a long time. Consider signet rings for sealing letters, which were used to verify the authenticity of a communication. More recently, key signing parties were started in the 1990s to tackle the digital version of this problem. Participants would print their own and others' digital key signatures and bring them in person to an event. Individuals then partnered up and verified each other's keys, making sure that they had the same ones. This method is similar to how Snowden verified Poitras' encryption key above, but was done in person with printouts. This made it possible for participants to communicate digitally and to trust that the digital person they were talking to was the actual person they had met at the key signing party.

In all digital messaging systems recommended in this book, there are ways to verify identities. Below is an example of the verification screen in Signal messenger on an iPhone. In this image, the application is asking you to check with the other person and to confirm that they see the same code on their device. If they do see the same code, then you can verify that you are safely talking to them and not someone pretending to be them.

Screenshot of identity verification screen in Signal.

After the revelations by Edward Snowden in 2013, a number of fake Edward Snowden and Glenn Greenwald Twitter accounts sprung up, perhaps hoping to discredit their work or attract others to communicate with them accidentally.[182] As you are searching for partners, double-check to make sure that you have the right account and not an imposter. A simple way to do this is to look at contact information (including messaging application usernames) that is listed publicly on their supposed organization's website. If you can't find this, take all initial messages with a grain of salt until you can verify that a person's identity.

Bad verification practices are seen constantly on the internet, and this can be a huge issue in the process of first contact. In the case of John Doe, there was no verification done (at least that has been publicly documented). It is possible that someone could have set up a fake account for Obermayer—essentially creating a honeypot, or an attractive false means of contact, for unsuspecting would-be sources. If one falls into such a trap, the entire process can be compromised during the initial contact. This technique is basically a digital sting operation.

When speaking about his communication practices with Doe in a 2016 interview with *Wired*, Obermayer explained that they used a variety of encrypted channels, switching messaging systems often and always clearing the history during the switch. He also spoke about their verification methods, noting that with each new communication channel the two would reauthenticate. "I'd say 'is it sunny?' You'd say 'the moon is raining' or whatever nonsense, and then both of us can verify it's still the other person on the device," said Obermayer.[183] Switching between communication channels can be a great way to make it harder to have your communications compromised, but you should always remember to reverify each other.

One easy method for verification is voice. If you've decided to allow your partner to know your identity, then you can use a secure voice channel to verify that the person on the other end is the same person you were talking to before. All secure messengers recommended in this book have an encrypted calling option. But there are some new ways to clone a person's voice, so be careful. In 2018, Baidu's Deep Voice software could clone a voice with only 3.7 seconds of training material, so it is possible for someone to put a fake voice on the other end. In general, unless your adversary is a state actor, using voice to verify each other is generally safe, as long as you don't need to be anonymous.

Revealing Your Identity

If the information you are providing is directly related to your identity, for instance if you are the victim of sexual harassment, there may be no way around telling your partner who you are. If your identity is the only way to confirm or deny the authenticity of the information, it will be hard to remain anonymous forever. That being said, you can always start anonymous, and then reveal your identity later on. There is no reason to do so from the start. Talk with your partner about the pros and cons of their knowing your identity. Usually there will be more cons, but in some particular circumstances there could be a need to reveal your identity to your partner. Doing so can also be a way to increase trust.

Obermaier says that he uses humor as a verification tool with sources. Though someone might be able to imitate someone else's writing style, it is hard to imitate someone else's humor. As with any relationship, the more time you've spent with someone, the more you should be able to verify that they are the same person based on their habits and affect. Add non sequiturs into conversations and see if you get the response you think they would give. If you establish this type of system from the beginning of a relationship, you can make it stronger against attacks.

A number of technical solutions can be used to try to simplify challenges related to digital verification and trust. Keybase.io has become a popular solution and is used by many security-minded individuals. It is similar to a social network, but each user must publicly verify ownership of their own social media accounts, email addresses, and websites. For example, my profile on keybase.io has been verified using my GitHub and Twitter accounts, my email address, and the control of my personal website. In this way, if someone is trying to reach out to me, they can be sure that the information listed on any of those services is indeed owned and controlled by me. Potential partners should set up their accounts similarly, making it easier for would-be sources and tipsters to trust that they are actually contacting who they think they are.

Timing

Though you may feel an urgency to stand up and reveal the truth immediately, in most cases it's much better not to rush in. Be methodical in your actions and have patience when it comes to communications with a partner.

In her statement given during her court martial, Chelsea Manning noted that she had a five-minute phone call with a reporter at the *Washington Post* and left a voice message for the public editor at the *New York Times* in early 2010, but that neither organization pursued this initial contact. This ultimately led Manning to work with WikiLeaks, largely because they had online messaging and submission systems. This gave her something closer to a real-time response to her inquiry.[184]

Systems for contacting journalists have evolved since 2010, and now most media outlets have online systems for communicating securely with would-be tipsters. This makes it more likely that your tip will be responded to in a timely manner.

Media agencies have also learned that they need to respond faster so that they don't lose stories. Of course, some organizations receive so many tips that they just don't have enough human power to efficiently sift through them. Organizations are also adopting more secure systems, which is good. The downside is that currently these systems are time-consuming for journalists to use. SecureDrop, for example, is complicated to check, involving two computers and transferring encrypted messages to air-gapped viewing stations. If this sounds cumbersome, it is.

Whoever you ultimately decide to contact, remember to be patient. This is a difficult decision that you are making and it takes courage to reach out. So take your time, be methodical, and set your expectations low for your first response. Journalists, lawyers, and other parties are busy and have other projects that they are already working on, just like any other person. A message from someone you don't know can easily slip through the cracks and be missed. Though you may want an immediate response, temper your expectations and wait a bit before you give up on your recipient and reach out to someone else. Sending a follow-up message can't hurt.

"Both sides need to be patient," says Obermaier. "It takes time for me to double-check the information. That's sometimes very hard to tell the other side, that this is not a lack of trust but a question of responsibility."

There can also be protection gained by increasing the time between information-gathering and disclosure. This can potentially make it harder for you to be identified. "Give the trail a chance to blow leaves over itself," says Gerard Ryle of the ICIJ. Timing can give you an advantage, so be sure to consider waiting on something instead of releasing it immediately.

On the flip side, if you have a piece of information that is incredibly time-sensitive, get it out. If the information you have is connected to an upcoming vote or an event, then you must get to a partner ASAP. You can even reach out to multiple partners at the same time and see who returns your message. Be sure you do this from a different pseudonymous account for each contact, and do not cross-contaminate them. Also, be upfront with any would-be partner you contact about the fact that you are reaching out to multiple potential partners. This can increase the trust in your relationship. Another reason to move quickly would be if you are currently being retaliated against. If this is the case, get a lawyer immediately. Again—it can't be emphasized enough—in almost all circumstances, having a lawyer can only be beneficial to you.

But in most circumstances, the release of information is not that time-sensitive, and it is better to give your contact time to respond instead of moving on to another potential partner. This can be a good first step in establishing trust between partners.

One last note on timing: sometimes the crimes you are disclosing have a certain date after which they will not be punishable. That was just the case with Amanda Schmitt, who accused Knight Landesman, the former publisher of Artforum, of sexual harassment. Schmitt was among the first of dozens of women who came forward to accuse Landesman, but because she did so five years after her employment, the judge dismissed her case. "The five-year gap between [Schmitt's] employment and the alleged wrongful acts is sufficient to eliminate any nexus between her employment and the alleged acts," the judge declared.[185] [186] If the statute of limitations is close to running out, move swiftly but with safety in mind.

Communication Style

When writing emails or messages, do not refer to yourself or provide details about yourself unless necessary. The less information you include about your identity, the better. Remember you are trying to be anonymous, or at least pseudonymous. That said, strategically hinting at reasons why a potential partner should trust you can be effective in convincing them to work with you. Such was the case in Snowden's pseudonymous email to Laura Poitras, in which he referred to himself as a "senior government employee in the intelligence community."

Try to consider what pieces of your communications could reveal aspects of your identity. Timing can be an easy giveaway of location and perhaps your lifestyle. Do you always write in the morning before work? Does when you communicate tell the recipient where you are located in the world? Consider changing the timing of your communications to obfuscate pieces of your identity.

Above all else, you need to be careful how you write, particularly with regard to the language that you use. Everyone has their own writing style and algorithms can now be used to identify writing samples. This is called stylometry and is used to compare language usage from multiple sources to determine how likely it is that a writing sample was written by a particular person. So be careful about your phrases and constructions. Your words can easily point the finger at you. On the other hand, if you deliberately add some stylistic red herrings, your words can potentially deflect the heat away from you.

Why should you be careful about how you write? Take the last paragraph as an example. The first sentence of that paragraph contains "particularly with regard to." This can be a hallmark of a writing style, and it would be better if it were changed. Everyone has tics in their writing and vocabulary that they use more often than others might, no matter how practiced they might be at editing and reediting their own words. One way to help eliminate such style quirks is to pass text through language translation software and then back again.

Here is the previous paragraph again, but translated into Korean, Arabic, Bosnian, then finally English once more.

Why should I be careful about how to write? For example, consider the last paragraph. The first sentence of the paragraph contains "special interest." This can be a feature of the write method, which is better if you change it. They all have characters in words and vocabulary that write more often than others, no matter how they edit and rearrange their words. One way to help solve these style problems is to transmit text through a language translation program and then return.

The translated paragraph isn't perfect—notably, it leaves out the word "stylometry"—but it gets the point across. Consider translation as a form of obfuscation for your communication to protect your identity.

Practical Communication Techniques

There are a number of ways to communicate with a partner, all with their own pros and cons. In-person meetings are OK as long as you are comfortable with not being anonymous to your partner and are aware of the ways that your location may be tracked. Normal phone calls are not secure. Postal mail is okay for reaching out to a partner, but be sure to do it anonymously. Do not use email, except for initial contact, and do so only with a throwaway account. Email is not safe for continued conversations, only for an anonymous first contact. Secure messaging applications are recommended, but you should research which ones will best protect you and then use them only from an anonymous device. Systems designed specifically for anonymous tips like SecureDrop are fantastic, but be ready for a slow pace of communication. Weigh your options carefully.

Before creating any accounts, make sure you are doing so from an anonymous web access point like a computer at the library, an anonymous tablet, or by using Tails on a laptop. Lots of messaging systems are available for pseudonymous communication, but be sure you are always using a device that is disconnected from your true identity. This is the most basic way to compartmentalize your communications with a partner.

By having a separate device, you can also make it harder for your adversaries to attack the devices of you or your partner. By breaking the security of digital devices or messaging applications, those in power can spy on the communication of those challenging them. A simple example is a corporation monitoring employee emails. In the U.S., these emails are generally considered "company property." Again, do not use work computers or email accounts when trying to communicate with a partner.

A recent global example of monitoring came from Citizen Lab's multi-year investigation into the Israeli-based "cyber warfare" vendor NSO Group. Their spyware, dubbed Pegasus, was created for hacking phones to enable the remote monitoring of individuals.[187] At the time of writing, Citizen Lab estimated that the spyware was being actively used in 45 countries. Pegasus is a bundle of "zero-day" exploits that, once installed, enables an operator to remotely control and observe a target's phone. This type of spyware gets sold to governments and organizations all over the world for monitoring those that try to challenge them. In particular, human rights activists and journalists have been targeted by these types of systems.

In May 2017, Javier Valdez Cárdenas, an award-winning journalist who was known for investigating cartels, was gunned down near his office in Culiacán, Sinaloa, Mexico. Two days later, a number of his colleagues' phones were targeted with phishing attacks with links to the Pegasus software. If the links had been opened, this spyware would have jeopardized the security of their phones and communications.[188] This is an extreme example, but it should make it clear that you can't always trust your personal device.

You need to have a separate digital device that isn't connected to your true identity. If you are ever publicly identified or your true identity is compromised, having an anonymous device is a great backup. This will make sure that the communications and activities that happened through it remain disconnected from you.

In Person

Before we jump straight into digital techniques, let's take a step back and look at other ways you could get in contact with a partner. The oldest and perhaps easiest way to quickly establish trust and a relationship is through an in-person meeting—by talking face-to-face. Clearly this is not anonymous, but if you have thought through your risks and decided that anonymity isn't a priority for you (perhaps you have been harassed or are being retaliated against and need a lawyer immediately), then face-to-face communication might be the best option.

"I, in many cases, still feel safest when I can have a walk with a person," says Frederik Obermaier. By taking the time to build a relationship, both parties can feel more comfortable sharing and planning a strategy together.

Setting up a meeting with someone face-to-face without leaving a trace is difficult and usually requires reaching out digitally first. Of course, you could go directly to a potential partner's workplace and wait outside or ask to see them without revealing your identity. However, if trying to remain anonymous is important to you, going to the New York Times Building in person is not a good option. Instead, consider reaching out via the mail.

John Cook suggests that one way to anonymously set up an initial in-person meeting with someone, particularly an investigative journalist, is to send them an anonymous letter with a time and place to meet, to write that you have important information, and then simply to go to that place and see if they show up. This might not be the fastest or highest-probability way to get in touch with someone, but it can be done relatively safely. Like postal mail, an anonymous email can be used to reach out to a potential partner and to ask for an in-person meeting.

If you have established communication and are now preparing to meet face-to-face with your partner, do a risk assessment and weigh the merits of a number of locations. Talk with your partner about where to meet. Choose a place that isn't near either of your homes, workplaces, or locations that you frequent: you don't want to be recognized. Also consider a place where you will blend in with the crowd.

Email Accounts

A new email address should be created whenever you are going to communicate with someone. This is a simple technique to compartmentalize your identity, thereby protecting yourself. If one account is compromised, it won't affect your other accounts or conversations.

Of the many potential secure email providers to use, many in the security community have had good luck with ProtonMail. Created by former scientists at CERN and MIT, ProtonMail has baked end-to-end encryption into its email system.

Email Encryption

Encrypted email is generally achieved by using a computer program that implements Pretty Good Privacy and turns your regular clear-text email messages into coded versions. These encoded versions can only be decoded and read by the person for whom you encrypted the email. For email encryption to work, both parties—the sender and the recipient—must be using PGP and must be well-practiced in doing so. This is very cumbersome. Even those who use encryption daily often make mistakes. The most common issue is accidentally sending an email without encrypting it, allowing all of the message content to flow through the standard email protocols. According to David Huerta, a digital security trainer at the Freedom of the Press Foundation, the basic PGP email encryption workflow is like "if you had to drive a car every day and you had to always remember to turn on the switch that says 'Don't Blow Up' halfway through." So don't use PGP email encryption. Instead, use ProtonMail, which implements PGP encryption automatically, though this only works if both you and the recipient are using the ProtonMail system. Even better, skip email altogether.

Riseup is another popular privacy-focused provider. It is a set of tools for email, chat, and document collaboration that is supported by a community of activists. Riseup requires that new users apply to use its services (which can take a while) or have a referral code (which can be hard to obtain if you don't know the right person). It also has its services hosted in the United States, which might be an issue for some users. In this book we focus on using ProtonMail to set up a pseudonymous email account.

To set up ProtonMail, use your anonymous tablet and connect to Tor or a VPN. Always do this before you proceed to send email or sign up for an email account. You must be consistent in your usage of Tor or a VPN.

On the anonymous tablet, install the ProtonMail application from the Google Play Store or by going to https://protonmail. com. Follow the "Sign Up" prompts to create a new account. The system will attempt to confirm that you are an actual human, not a spambot trying to create random accounts. Typically a captcha is used to confirm your humanity, but sometimes if you are connecting to the site using Tor or a VPN, the captcha method might not be available.

If you do not see an option to use a captcha, try connecting from a different Wi-Fi location or from a different VPN server or different Tor route. Do not use text verification to verify your humanity, because this will link the email address to your phone number.

Whenever you create a new email account, memorize the username and password, or better yet, store it in a password manager.

Do not cross-contaminate your email accounts. Use one email account per service or per conversation. Keep your accounts compartmentalized.

The main downside to email is that a history of the communication will always exist, whether on email provider servers, on your or your partner's devices, or even through a log of metadata gathered by a government or corporation. If possible, always choose a secure messenger over email, because it leaves less of a data trail.

Email is not a recommended communication technique!

Foldering

Just in case you've heard of this before, it's important to let you know that foldering is not a safe mode of communication. It is a generalized term for communicating via saved drafts in an online system, where one party logs into a webmail account and writes a message and saves it as a draft, then the other party logs into the same webmail account and reads the draft, then deletes it. David Petraeus, former director of the CIA, and Paula Broadwell, his biographer, used this technique to try to keep their messages—and their affair—secret. More recently Paul Manafort was accused of using this technique to hide his communications.[189] Note that foldering is not illegal in itself; it all depends on what the messages are and how they are used. It is not recommended, though, because it doesn't offer much protection, especially compared to other secure communication messaging services.

Instant Messengers

Aside from email, a number of other options are available for communicating pseudonymously and securely online. A growing list of instant messenger applications claim to be private and secure, including iMessage, Google Hangouts, WhatsApp, Keybase.io, Telegram, Riot.im, Wire, Wickr, Signal, Threema, and many more. I have been following the trajectory and usage of these applications for a number of years, and currently two stand above the rest (at least in the United States): Wire and Signal. These are recommended here for both pseudonymous and everyday communications. Remember, just like all messenger applications, Wire and Signal can only be used securely when both parties are using them, so make sure your partner has the same application as you or get them to adopt a new one.

Do Your Own Research

Technology is constantly changing, and recommendations can shift quickly. It is up to you to do more research about which messaging system you should be using. The Electronic Frontier Foundation actually stopped updating their secure messenger recommendation scorecard in 2018. Not only are there a lot of applications to keep up with, the pros and cons also depend heavily on the user's exact context. For example, Wire might hypothetically work well for a user in Switzerland, but be a red flag for a user in Myanmar (not that this is actually the case, but each user will certainly have a specific context and use case to take into consideration). The EFF now hosts a series of articles that explain how to research and decide what the best messenger might be for your particular use case.[190] So if you are reading this book in 2029 or in China, the standard for a secure messenger between partner and source might not be what is recommended here.

Use your anonymous research techniques to empower yourself so that you can be confident in your decisions. The Electronic Frontier Foundation and the Tactical Technology Collective are good starting points for more research. Keep the following questions in mind when assessing whether a communication tool is right for you:

- Are messages encrypted?
- Where and how is the content and metadata of your messages stored and secured?

- Are there retention policies that describe when metadata is destroyed from logs?
- Has the tool been externally audited?
- Is the tool open-source? Can anyone review the code?
- Can message histories be easily deleted?
- Does the party you are trying to contact already have this tool?
- Does your adversary have the power to access your content or metadata more readily if you choose one tool over another?
- Will the use of this tool be a red flag, making you stand out?
- Are web links auto-downloaded and previewed, and if so, could this identify you?[191]

Here are the reasons why Signal and Wire are recommended:

- Both are open-source and have had their code bases audited by third parties.
- Both limit log retention (how long they keep any records that your device connected to their servers). This makes it harder for others even with a subpoena to discover your identity or access your messages or metadata.
- Both have privacy-focused features like "disappearing messages," which enables messages to delete themselves after they have been delivered.
- Both strip the metadata and location out of photos when they are sent, limiting ways that extra tracking information could inadvertently slip through.

- Both offer encrypted voice communication, meaning that you can make calls through these applications and no one else can snoop on what you are saying through your connection.

Voice Communication

Standard text messages and cell phone calls are insecure and should be avoided. There are special devices routinely used by law enforcement and others to track, record, and even block standard texting and calls from mobile devices.[192] These standard communication protocols leave a bounty of metadata and the messages themselves on servers for potentially years, making collection without your knowledge relatively simple.[193] [194] The release of documents by Edward Snowden showed that the NSA and GHCQ worked together to secretly infiltrate and steal the global encryption keys for a majority of the world's cell phone SIM cards, making nearly all cell phone calls and text messages potentially readable by these agencies.[195] Landlines have historically been tapped and eavesdropped on by governments and should be avoided. Do not use standard voice communication systems. Instead, use the encrypted voice options in the secure messengers listed here.

Wire

I recommend Wire for one particular reason: unlike Signal, Wire requires only an email address to sign up, not a phone number. It is easy to create an anonymous email address, but quite difficult to create and maintain a phone number completely anonymously. Even if you were to use a burner phone to register Signal, the phone would still ping cell towers whenever you turned it on. If someone knew your phone number from Signal, they could potentially use it to track your present and past locations. By using an email address to sign up, Wire makes it easy to have multiple accounts, allowing for further compartmentalization of identities and anonymous activities.

"Wire Personal" is available for Android, iOS, Windows, macOS, and Linux, so you should have no trouble setting it up on your anonymous device. Wire also works on a tablet, something that isn't currently possible with Signal. Of course, no matter where you are using Wire, be sure to connect to Tor or a VPN first before starting it.

In terms of legal protections, the company behind Wire is located in privacy-friendly Switzerland, with servers in Ireland and Germany. This potentially makes it more difficult for anyone to gain access to your data or metadata through legal means. Additionally, messages sent with Wire are stored, encrypted, on company servers and can only be decrypted by the recipient of the message, not by the company.[196]

Before launching Wire or any messaging application, make sure you are connected to a VPN or Tor. To get started, sign up for an account with a pseudonymous email address. Make sure you: 1) use "timed messages," that is, messages that auto-destroy after the receiver reads them and 2) disable link previews, as these can be used by adversaries to track you.[197]

It is important to note that like many startups, Wire has had to figure out how to make money. Recently Wire launched "Wire Pro," which falls into the team collaboration category of software, much like Slack. If this direction continues and Wire abandons

"Wire Personal," it would no longer function as an effective tool for anonymous communication.

Video Calls

As for video calls, skip them for now. They are not anonymous. If you really need to make a video call, Wire has a built-in video implementation using WebRTC. Jitsi is another free web-based system that is encrypted for one-on-one calls. At the time of writing, there is no open-source end-to-end encrypted system for video calls that is recommended.

Setting Up Signal Anonymously

Signal is currently more popular in the U.S. than Wire, so if you can't find a partner on Wire, you will likely find them on Signal. Unfortunately, setting up Signal anonymously is a bit cumbersome, because it requires an anonymous phone number to register. To do this in a secure way, you will need two anonymous phones: 1) a smartphone that will never be registered with a phone number and doesn't have a SIM card and 2) a simple flip phone that will be registered anonymously with a phone number. The flip phone will be used only to receive one verification text from the Signal servers, then never used again.

Acquiring a phone number anonymously can be difficult in some countries, but it is surprisingly easy in the U.S. Pay-as-you-go services such as Boost Mobile, Cricket Wireless, or Tracfone support this. You can buy phones and SIM cards for these services from big-box stores such as Best Buy, Walmart, or

Target. Again, make sure when buying that you are as anonymous as possible, using all of the tips that we have already discussed. The phone's serial number and IMEI number will be
registered at the time and location it is sold to you. So wear a
disguise, pay cash, and don't bring your regular phone.

Once you have bought your two prepaid phones anonymously
(one smartphone and one flip phone) you should go to a place
that is not your home or anywhere you normally go. That way,
when you register the flip phone, your location transmitted to
the phone-company servers will not be associated with your true
identity. Again, no matter how hard it is to be disconnected for a
little while, make sure you don't have your real phone with you.

Your job now will be to register the flip phone, so that you can
get a phone number. Do not insert a SIM or register the smartphone; it will only be used over Wi-Fi, never connected to a cell
carrier. If possible, use a phone number that has an area code or
country code that does not match your normal location or use one
that will make you less unique.

The process for registration usually involves going to the carrier's website and using a prepaid top-up card to pay for the service. At this point, you will likely have to enter the phone's IMEI
number (this can be found under the battery) and the SIM card's
ICCID number. Remember to do this all from an anonymous
browser, as detailed previously.

Once you have a working flip phone, take the smartphone and
configure it similarly to the anonymous tablet, making sure you
immediately disable any location services in the phone settings.
This will disable all GPS and location data that might be determined via one's Wi-Fi connection.

Again, never register the smartphone with a SIM card. And always keep Airplane Mode turned on when using it. This will block your phone's baseband processor from communicating with your cellular provider. You should still be able to turn on Wi-Fi with Airplane Mode on.

Voice Over IP Phone Numbers

There are a number of services for acquiring phone numbers that can be used through the internet. Unfortunately, most of these require you to already have a phone number to register, and must be purchased with a credit card. If you want to create a more anonymous phone number, it is possible to register for a VoIP phone number using a burner phone, then register for another VoIP using the first one you created for verification, which can distance your true identity from the final phone number you will acquire. Be sure whenever signing up for a VoIP phone number to use Tor.

Set up Tor or a VPN and a password manager on the smartphone, then install Signal from the Google Play Store. Be sure to use Tor or a VPN when you sign up for Signal to obfuscate the IP address from which your account is created. Use the phone number of the anonymous flip phone to register Signal. A verification text message will be sent to the flip phone. Enter the verification code on the smartphone to complete your Signal installation.

It used to be that your Signal account would be secure only as long as you controlled the phone number associated with it, but recently Signal added a new feature to help ensure no one can hijack your account. Enable the "Registration Lock" setting under the privacy settings section. Now even if someone else registers their phone with your phone number—after, say, your flip phone number's registration lapses—no one can take over your Signal account.

Signal & Photos

Taking photos from within Signal will keep them in Signal and will never save to your phone itself, so you can be sure that the photo is destroyed if you turn on disappearing messages in Signal. This is a great way to get images of documents to a partner without creating a log of the photo on your device.

At the time of writing, Signal could not be installed on a tablet. If this does become an option in the future, it would be better to use a tablet than a smartphone. Smartphones still have a baseband processor that could potentially be a vector for attack if the phone is not kept in Airplane Mode.

One of the reasons that privacy advocates like Signal is that it doesn't store any more information on company servers than absolutely necessary. With regard to log files, the company keeps only the date of the first time you signed up, along with the date that your phone last connected to the servers. Many providers of secure messaging applications claim that they don't store or retain your data, but these types of claims are hard to confirm.

In the case of Signal, this extra care around data retention has been tested through subpoenas of user information by the U.S. government. Legally, Signal has to provide all information that it has available for a particular account when required by subpoena. As released documents have shown, Signal stores virtually no information and doesn't have logs to hand over to the government when demanded.[198] Looking at past government data requests is a great way to verify companies' privacy claims. This confirmation of Signal's dedication as a company to protecting its users makes it a strong choice for privacy.

Anonymous Tip Systems

Two projects have been created to streamline and secure the process of getting tips and information from sources to partners: SecureDrop and GlobaLeaks. Both are web-based and should be primarily accessed through Tor. Each uses a number of security methods, including physical air-gaps with SecureDrop, to secure and anonymize the identity of and information provided by a source.

SecureDrop is a project by the Freedom of the Press Foundation that allows organizations to offer a web-based secure tool for conversations and the passing of files from source to journalist completely anonymously. SecureDrop has been adopted mostly by media organizations such as the *New York Times, USA Today, Financial Times*, the Associated Press, and many others. SecureDrop is also gaining traction with public accountability organizations such as the Project on Government Oversight and ExposeFacts. Links to SecureDrop sites hosted by news organizations on the dark web can be found here: https://securedrop.org/directory.

GlobaLeaks is maintained by the Hermes Center for Transparency and Digital Human Rights. It differs from SecureDrop in that it strives to be more customizable per installation, allowing operators to find a balance between source anonymity and usability. GlobaLeaks has been adopted outside of media and public accountability organizations, namely by anti-corruption organizations and even by some city governments in Europe, such as the Barcelona City Council and the Italian National Anti-Corruption Authority. Even the company Edison in Italy is using it. Organizations that use GlobaLeaks can be found here: https://www.globaleaks.org/who-uses-it/.

In both systems there is no registration process, and you don't need an email address or phone number to log in. It is a completely anonymous process. Instead, once you submit a tip or upload a document, you are provided with a passphrase. This can then be used to return anonymously and check for messages from an operator or add more information to your tip. Because these systems are anonymous, there is no way for the system to contact you for an update; instead you must log back in and check for new responses. This can be taxing for the user, but it is a requirement for a truly anonymous system.

When using either of these services, be sure to research them first and to visit the systems only via Tor hidden services, a.k.a. the dark web. This makes it harder for your digital connection to these services to be traced back to you. For example, BuzzFeed's SecureDrop site is http://ndg43ilvrrj465ix.onion/, with the url ending in ".onion," which signifies that it is available through Tor. Remember, be sure to think about uniqueness when using Tor and SecureDrop or GlobaLeaks. Are you the only person at your IP address using Tor? Never do this from work and always use an anonymous device.

If contacting an organization through one of these systems, be patient. It might take a while to get a response. "It takes journalists a while to go through everything that comes through Secure-

Drop," says Trevor Timm, a co-founder and the executive director of the Freedom of the Press Foundation. Submission systems, notably SecureDrop, have been streamlined for the workflow of the source, making it relatively easy and incredibly safe to submit documents. Interacting with tip systems from within the recipient's organization is another reality. "[Journalists] are jumping through a bunch of hoops on the other side," says Timm. Just to view a document submitted over SecureDrop, as previously noted, a journalist has to reboot two different computers into a special operating system and use multiple layers of encryption and decryption. So have respect and patience for the energy that your potential partner is putting into protecting you. Note that at the time of writing, SecureDrop is being updated to make it easier for operators to use, which should speed up the response time.

One of the biggest advantages of these systems over secure messengers is that hardly any metadata can be collected. The metadata that is created is encrypted. With SecureDrop, the metadata and information is stored on a server on the organization's premises, making it harder for authorities to legally gather material. Secure messengers, on the other hand, can have metadata stored on servers owned by the messaging system, and there can always be material on a partner's device. "You have to rely on the reporter to delete the conversations from the phone. If they don't, if they keep the number in there, then the facts of the communication channel are pretty easy for law enforcement to deduce," says John Cook, investigations editor at *Business Insider* and former editor-in-chief of *The Intercept.*

Though both systems create a strong base level of security for the source, this doesn't remove the need for you to think through your actions. Be sure to use the best practices we outlined earlier when messaging through these systems, and always use Tor when connecting to them. Don't fall into the trap of just assuming that you can drop off information into these systems anonymously and expect it to have an impact. You need to be responsible for the material that you are providing. Create a relationship with the operator on the other side, and move to one of the secure messengers written about here if that is what you and your partner decide. SecureDrop and GlobaLeaks are simply other tools to be used in the process of revealing the truth, but there is no quick fix, so weigh your options carefully.

Data Delivery

The simplest and safest way to deliver information to a partner is using a secure messenger. Of course, sometimes this isn't that simple—for instance, if you need to send files that are too large to send over the application, or if the information you have isn't digital in the first place. There are a few ways to tackle this, some digital and some old-school. Be sure to discuss ways of doing this with your partner and use your risk assessment to determine the safest way to transfer information.

If the information is physical and not digital, there are a few ways of getting it to your partner. The simplest is to meet with them in person and hand it off. Obviously, that will not protect your identity. Your partner will know who you are. If you wish to be anonymous, you have two options. One is to mail the material to them without leaving any traces in the packaging or information itself. Or two, the classic spycraft option: a dead drop where they can pick it up later on, under a park bench, in a trash can, behind a loose brick. You get the idea.

All of these physical delivery techniques will also work for large digital files. If you can't send the files via a secure chat system, you can always put files on a USB flash drive and transfer it to your partner using one of the previous techniques. Of course, for extra security, be sure to encrypt the files or flash drive. Windows, Mac, and Linux all have options for encrypting flash drives and files so that they require a password to unlock. Start by researching more online, particularly the Freedom of the Press Foundation's easy-to-follow training materials: https://freedom.press/training/. Once your flash drive is encrypted, you can either dead-drop or mail the drive to your partner, and then you can send them a password through a messaging application.

An alternative to the physical drop-off method is to encrypt the files and then send them over a file-sharing system such as Google Drive, WeTransfer, or Dropbox. Micah Lee explains that this technique entails "uploading big encrypted files and then using SecureDrop to share the key." This should be done only if a) the file-hosting service is signed up for with a pseudonymous account using Tor, b) encryption is used, and c) you can be sure that your communication with your partner is secure. If all those things are done correctly this can be a "reasonable way of doing it," says Lee.

Note that if you are up against a strong adversary such as a state actor and you are being actively monitored, it is better to use something even more anonymous. In these circumstances, OnionShare is a great option. Developed and maintained by Lee, OnionShare can work only when both the source and the partner have their computers connected to Tor at the same time. OnionShare essentially starts a web server on the sharer's computer and creates a unique, unguessable web address such as http://xcuvaygdkvswo2ak.

onion/craziness-bunkbed. The sharer then sends this address to the recipient, and they visit the address with the Tor browser. This will then download the file to their computer. The sender can also see when the file has been transferred and OnionShare will nicely clean up after itself, automatically shutting down its sharing service after the file has been downloaded once. This is a great tool and should be used unless you are dealing with incredibly large files.[199]

There are many ways to transfer information to a partner. Just make sure you talk about the pros and cons of each one with your partner before you start. Be methodical. That's the best way to remain safe.

Screenshot of the OnionShare application
sharing a document over the Tor network.

Documentation Gathering, Sanitization, and Storage

Collection

As you collect documents and bring new information to light, be aware that you are in an escalating digital arms race. There will always be new ways that data forensics can identify you, or uncover information based on data that you inadvertently leave in your files, or data that is retained in logs noting who has accessed what files on what network. Recently it was discovered that noise from electrical grids can be used to quite accurately pinpoint when, and potentially where, an audio recording was made.[200] The best way to win this war—or at least to avoid becoming collateral damage—is to work outside the standard methods and find partners who have experience.

Of course, the actual collection of documents has changed dramatically over the years. In 1969, Daniel Ellsberg systematically removed documents, including the Pentagon Papers, from the RAND Corporation in his briefcase, taking them to an advertising agency where he (sometimes with the help of his 13-year-old son) photocopied them, one page at a time. Though this took enormous courage and psychological stamina—and in 1969 all that copying was certainly time-consuming and undoubtedly tiresome—it was also technologically straightforward and relatively safe. As long as the guards didn't stop and check his briefcase, and as long as no one saw him remove and return the reports, Ellsberg could duplicate the papers undetected.[201]

If Ellsberg was trying to do the same thing in 2019 with physical documents, he would have to be sure there weren't cameras looking over his shoulder. He would have to make sure that the documents themselves didn't have watermarks that would lead back to him. And he would have to make sure that the copying method didn't log his activity. If Ellsberg's 21st-century counterpart were to take digital documents, there would be many more potential technological risks and traps to avoid along the way.

Take Notes

Before you start collecting documents or even trying to tell anyone about the wrongs you want to expose, start documenting what you see. Jesselyn Radack, who heads the Whistleblower and Source Protection Program at ExposeFacts and has worked with Thomas Drake and Edward Snowden, says the first step is to "just keep your own little record at home in a little notebook." This should be a notebook where you methodically record everything pertinent to the wrongs you want to expose: everything that you see, everything that you hear, and everything that you say. Do this as often as you can, the same day that incidents occur. Note the time and date of each occurrence. Above all, your notes should always include any complaints you raise and to whom, as well as any retaliation against you for doing so.

This approach to notetaking played a critical role in the big Russian sports doping scandal in 2016. Grigory Rodchenkov, the whistleblower and former doctor of the Russian Olympic team, took incredibly detailed contemporaneous notes that became compelling evidence. The notes included Rodchenkov's interactions with Russian coaches, officials, and athletes, such as how and when he provided performance-enhancing drugs to athletes, and how the doping was hidden from Olympic observers and their drug tests. Aside from all of these incriminating notes, as the *New York Times* reported, Rodchenkov also noted his daily activities details such as "6:30, I took a shower, had a smoke, got ready, had hot cereal and farmer's cheese at breakfast." These seemingly trivial details helped convince the judges to allow the journal to be considered credible evidence in the court case.[202]

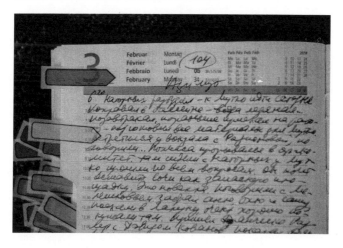

Detail of Rodchenkov's personal diary. © *Hilary Swift,* The New York Times

The technology you use to take notes can either help or hinder those who might seek to access and/or destroy any information you have, depending upon your situation. You can use a physical notebook, good old pen and paper, or notes on an anonymous laptop or tablet. But be sure to stay away from making entries at work or on your personal computer unless you are highly technically confident of your computer's security.

"Documentation is very important," says Debra Katz, founding partner of Katz, Marshall & Banks, LLP and the lawyer who represented Christine Blasey Ford when she was called to testify during the Kavanaugh confirmation hearings. "We increasingly have people who show up with videotapes of harassment. I've had clients who've had their iPhone rolling as their employer, predictably, would come in and do back massages or make sexual remarks." Logs of text messages on phones or even recordings of interactions can be crucial to demonstrating that harassment is taking place. Save logs of all of your conversations and interactions, because you never know how they might prove useful later on.

The text messages sent by Mike Isabella and partners to Chloe Caras (who was also represented by Debra Katz) were used as evidence in the lawsuit that eventually took down Mike Isabella Concepts restaurants for sexual harassment.[203] If you are going to attempt to record interactions as evidence, be sure that you are aware of the relevant recording laws. In some states and countries, you must inform the other party that you are recording and you must obtain their consent to be recorded. These laws are collectively known as two-party consent laws. Do more research into your context before you start shooting video or recording audio as documentation. You don't want your evidence thrown out of court. You don't want to be sued for releasing the recording. The Reporters Committee for Freedom of the Press is a good place to learn more about two-party consent laws in the United States.

Recommended Collection Approach

In New York City in 1953, a newspaper boy was finishing his day, jingling his coins around, when he noticed that one nickel felt lighter than the rest. When he dropped the coin on the floor, it split open, revealing a tiny photograph with numbers. This turned out to be microfilm that was destined for Soviet spy Reino Hayhanen.[204] In 1957, Hayhanen defected to the U.S., where he exposed the spycraft of the Soviets to the FBI. This included the use of microfilm and dead drops for communication. Though this example may seem far from the world of computers and smartphones, taking photos of documents with microfilm is much safer than taking the actual documents, in the same way taking a digital photo is safer than copying the digital document. In such a case, there is far less potential for a log of the interaction.

The current best way to gather information is by taking pictures of documents or computer screens using a pseudonymous digital device. This method effectively circumvents all of the normal digital surveillance systems that might come into play when you copy data off of a network or onto a USB stick (e.g., logs of the copying or digital watermarking). It also circumvents any logging software that may be installed on your computer. Company or government tracking software can record the actions of taking screenshots or other mouse and keyboard actions. Evidence from one of these loggers was used by the FBI against Terry Albury, an FBI field agent who was sent to jail for disclosing classified information to *The Intercept*. In an affidavit in support of the search warrant, the FBI cited a number of facts, including that Albury had "conducted cut and paste activity" while viewing one of the classified documents. This fact could only have been gathered by latent logging software installed on his computer or built into a viewing program.[205] By skipping digital copying or screenshotting, and instead simply taking a picture of the computer screen, you can circumvent some of these monitoring systems. Of course, if you are logged in and have a document open, you should assume that there is a log of the access as well.

Keep these tips in mind:

- Only use a pseudonymous device for taking photos; never use your personal or work device.
- Use a small tablet with Wi-Fi turned off instead of a phone; this way there will be no location information stored as metadata in the photos.[206]
- Make sure the photos don't have any identifying information in them; this could be your hand, your reflection on the computer screen, images of your office, or other identifying information or marks on your computer screen.
- Be sure to check the images afterwards for any metadata or accidental information captured, and make sure to sanitize the images if necessary.
- Audio and video recordings can potentially replace taking photos, but these types of files can be harder to sanitize.
- Be sure there aren't video cameras that could capture you in the act of taking photos.

Microdots

Do not trust printers. Color laser jet printers and copiers embed metadata in the documents that they print in the form of microdots, which are patterns of tiny yellow dots that are almost invisible to the naked eye. These dots encode information, similar to QR codes. This includes the printer's serial number, the time and date, the network address, and potentially other information. This data can be used to pinpoint when and where documents were printed, and potentially by whom. If you want to find out more on the topic, research the terms "printer steganography" and "machine identification code."

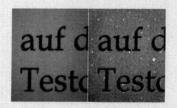

Regular and enhanced image of a printed page from an HP Color LaserJet 3700 showing yellow microdots. Photography by Florian Heise, Druckerchannel.de, in the public domain via Wikimedia Commons

Copying Digital Files

It is nearly impossible to copy files to a USB stick without leaving a trace, particularly if you are using log-in credentials at work or on a company device. Computers and networks are built to track and log file access, transfers, and printing. Do not try to make a digital transfer or to copy information onto a USB stick at work unless you can be positive that this process isn't being logged somewhere. Use the Tails operating system, or a computer that is offline, when you copy data.

If you must copy digital files, be sure to collect all your information as anonymously as possible: use a shared computer at work (not your own). Do not use your own login credentials. Also, consider your physical location. It is best not to attempt this in your own office, for instance. Gathering information in the office will become even less viable as technology and employee surveillance software evolves.

Aside from the issues around copying digital files, some sensitive documents (particularly from government agencies) come with "phone home" beacons embedded in them or with digital rights management built in, making it impossible to view or print documents if you aren't logged in. This could be a remote image or link embedded in a document, such that when you view the document, the image pings back to a server owned by the government or creator of the document. This allows the creator to see the IP address and potentially more information about you as a viewer. Microsoft files such as Word documents have been known to have "locating beacons" placed within them.[207] PDFs may also include this type of beacon, though Adobe now tries to notify users before documents call a remote server. To combat this type of tracking, either convert a document to a safe format such as plain text with the command line, or view a document on a computer that is "air-gapped," meaning that it is not connected to the internet. Make it impossible for your adversary to know you have the documents.

Uniqueness and Backflushing

If you are one of a limited number of individuals with access to the information you are releasing, then no matter how careful you are, it will be easy to trace you. This was the case with Reality Winner. In the criminal complaint filed against Winner, the FBI noted that only six individuals had accessed the document that was disclosed to *The Intercept*.[208] When this document showed up on the website, the FBI had six individuals to start investigating, including Winner. Her unique trail quickly made her the most likely suspect. One way to combat uniqueness is by increasing the number of individuals who have access to a document before it is released.

Danielle Brian, executive director of the Project on Government Oversight, described a method that has been in use in D.C. for years: "backflushing." Before disclosing a document, send it through official channels to as many legitimate places as possible. For example, include the document in a report and send the report to other departments. This makes it so others have the document as well, vastly reducing the uniqueness of your connection to the document. When you disclose the information later on, it will not be clear that you were in any way connected to it.

Another way to combat uniqueness is by gathering the data through a shared digital account, e.g., if someone else is logged into a computer and you copy a file while they are logged in, the document-gathering will be connected to them, not you. Of course, this should be done carefully and ethically, so as not to inadvertently cast blame on someone else. If possible, it's better to hijack a shared network account. So consider how unique the connection between the information and your identity might be. There is protection to be gained by hiding in the crowd.

Theft and Misfiling

Corporations sometimes lash back at whistleblowers by filing criminal charges for theft of company property. So be aware that by taking documents off company property, you may open yourself up to a legal battle.[209] This was one reason that SOC, a government security contractor, gave for firing Jennifer Glover, a security guard who had been sexually assaulted and harassed at work. Her termination letter stated that Glover had used her smartphone to take a photograph of the daily schedule, an act that they viewed as justifying her termination.[210] [211]

As an alternative to taking physical or digital documents, consider the misfiling technique. Hide copies of documents at work, either by misnaming digital files or by storing physical copies or USB sticks somewhere at work. In the future, you can "stumble upon" the copies, providing investigators with the information. They, not you, would then be removing property from company premises. The bottom line is that it might be helpful to have a backup copy of any important material stashed somewhere at work.

Sanitization

Sanitization is the process of removing, concealing, or cleaning up information in documents before you give them to someone else. Whether the documents you're dealing with are physical or digital, images or videos, the same general process applies: you should overwrite, obscure, or remove any sensitive information. This process is ubiquitous the world over in redacting classified material to prepare it for release to the public. When attempting this, imagine that you are in a heist film: be meticulous, wear gloves, wipe down surfaces to remove fingerprints, and don't leave anything that contains your DNA.

For those who are trying to disclose information, the process of sanitization is a little more complex, but there are two goals: 1) the removal of any information that could identify you, such as fingerprints, email addresses, or unique watermarks on documents; and 2) the removal of sensitive information that might harm someone else or have undue consequences if released, such as any company or government secrets or any personally identifiable information. This is where ethics and judgment come into play. Who would be harmed if this information were released? You don't want to accidentally victimize (or revictimize) a colleague, accidentally reveal personal information that could compromise one's reputation, or put a field agent in harm's way.

To sanitize physical items with nonporous surfaces, such as USB sticks or hard drives, wipe them down with a cleaning product and towel. Paper documents and other porous surfaces are more difficult to sanitize. There are a number of techniques for attempting this, but most involve using an eraser and potentially a cornstarch mixture to remove any oils left by fingerprints.[212] If you are providing someone with a device such as a hard drive, remove any serial numbers or identifying information that would make that product traceable, and of course, be sure to pay cash when buying any hardware that you might use.[213] If you must provide physical documents, redact them first with a black marker or white-out and then photocopy them, providing a redacted copy instead of the original.

For digital documents, the process of sanitization can be broken down into two strategies: 1) redaction, the process of obfuscating information within a document; and 2) metadata removal, the process of deleting identifying traces from the document.

Text

Any text-based document (rich text files, DOC and DOCX formats, CSVs, Microsoft Excel files, PowerPoint files, Adobe InDesign files, etc.) should first be converted to a PDF. This can be done on most computers with either "print to PDF" or "export to PDF" functionality. The PDF should then be opened, and each page should be exported as an image and then redacted in image-editing software. Draw black boxes over areas of sensitive or identifying information in the images. Note: If you try to redact the documents from within the PDF, it will be done in layers, leaving the actual data underneath the black boxes. This will not technically remove the sensitive information.[214] Similarly, it is important to use only image formats that do not include layers. If layers are included, someone can later remove the redaction layer and see the sensitive information underneath. JPG is a great image format to use, as it cannot save layers. After all of the images have been edited, they should be either recombined into a new PDF using a PDF viewer or given to someone as a set of images.

An alternative option is to use PDF Redact Tools, which automates those processes for you.[215] It is currently available on Linux or macOS and comes bundled inside the Tails operating system.

Images

Images should be redacted just the same as text documents. Save them in a format without layers such as a JPG. Draw black boxes over any portions that need to be removed, then save them.

Video and Audio

Redaction of video and audio files can be a bit trickier, but the same basic process of obfuscating information applies. For videos, open them in a video editing program and either delete portions of the video or add black boxes over sensitive pieces. Then export the edited video. Audio files should be edited in an audio editor (Audacity is a good free choice), and portions of the recordings can be deleted or replaced with a standard sine wave tone (like a censorship bleep).

Remember, though, that there may be other information in audio and video recordings that isn't obvious at first glance. Is there background noise or imagery that can be analyzed to determine the time and place it was taken? Are there reflections or other subtle pieces of data that could compromise you or someone else? Be very careful when it comes to audio and video, because so much information is contained in each file that it can be hard to think of every single thing that should be redacted.

Metadata Removal

Of course, if you are simply trying to get a video out, but trying to make it less obvious who it was shot by, removing the underlying capture information might be all that's needed. This is where removing metadata comes into play.

For example, the metadata embedded in a photo taken with a smartphone might contain the model of the phone, the time it was taken, and possibly the location of the phone at the time of capture (if GPS location was enabled). This data needs to be removed if you are trying to make the photo, video, or any other type of file untraceable.

Before anything else, check the filename for anything that could identify you or your means of creating the image. If you have any doubt—rename it.

All digital files inherently contain some distinct information that identifies them: filename, creation date and time, last modified date and time, and file size. Some digital file formats contain even more information. Microsoft Word documents, for example, are known for automatically saving additional metadata, such as the authors who worked on the document and the names and locations of the computers where the file was saved. Unfortunately, with these documents and particularly with proprietary file formats, it might be difficult or near-impossible to remove all pieces of metadata. Instead, convert proprietary formats to simple open-source formats that have consistent metadata formatting.

Some file formats use standard data wrappers to store metadata, such as EXIF (exchangeable image file format) or XMP (Extensible Metadata Platform). These are used for almost all image formats and PDFs. By converting other documents into these formats, it becomes much easier to delete metadata and know that it is really gone.

To actually remove metadata from an image, a PDF, or a video file, open it with its corresponding editing software and look for options such as "Properties," "Inspector," or "Document Inspector." This should open up a dialog with a list of all of the metadata fields and entries. Delete them all. You will also want to research format-specific metadata removal methods for specific file types. Audio and video files, such as MP3s or MP4s, for example, can have proprietary ID3 tags embedded within them—such as PRIV frames—that make it near impossible to know if they have been sanitized.[216]

Alternatively, a number of applications can scrub metadata from particular file formats. Several applications can remove EXIF data from images, but the Android application "EZ UnEXIF Free (EXIF Remover)" is especially useful for those communicating via an anonymous smartphone or tablet. This application removes all EXIF data, including geolocation, from photos taken with an Android device.

The Metadata Anonymisation Toolkit (MAT) provides a simple interface for stripping metadata from a number of formats, including PNG, JPEG, PDF, MP3, and Microsoft Office Document formats. MAT comes installed on Tails. However, MAT currently hasn't been updated since January 2016, essentially making it abandonware. Fortunately, MAT2, the replacement for MAT, is under active development and currently in beta. This is a great tool that can be used to sanitize a variety of files, but please check on its current development status online before using it.[217] [218]

Storage

Be cautious about where you store documentation. Never store documentation at work, unless you are following the misfiling method mentioned previously. You may feel that your desk or office is a safe space, but it isn't. You can consider storing documents at home, but this is an obvious choice for all concerned. In many cases, those who are trying to disclose information have had their houses ransacked and searched by their adversaries, both legally and illegally. If a subpoena is filed, information in your home will not be protected.

A good strategy is to either store documents outside your home or office or give a backup copy of what you will be revealing to a trusted person for safekeeping. Daniel Ellsberg gave a copy of a classified nuclear study to his brother, who hid the documents under a large gas stove in a garbage dump.[219] Unfortunately, while this protected them for a while, the documents were ultimately destroyed by water damage, and Ellsberg spent years trying to reconstitute the information they contained. Instead of your brother, choose a lawyer. In the United States, information stored with your attorney may be protected from search and seizure through attorney-client privilege. Of course, there are exceptions to this, which was the case in the raid on the office of President Trump's former attorney Michael Cohen. If investigators can make the case that attorney-client privilege is being used "in furtherance of a contemplated or ongoing crime or fraud," then they will be able to search a lawyer's office under the crime-fraud exception.[220] [221]

All digital documentation should be stored on either encrypted USB drives or on an encrypted pseudonymous device, such as an encrypted tablet or a Tails USB drive. Documents should never be stored in the cloud or on a personal computer or device.

Scenarios

This section comprises a series of hypothetical situations in which you might find yourself. Read through these scenarios with an eye toward the real threats and risks you may face, what your standard response might be, and what an informed anonymous and secure response might be. You might be tempted to see the technologically sophisticated strategies as the better options. Remember, the tactics used to protect yourself should be determined by the threats and the situation, not by assuming that more technology is necessarily more secure. Sometimes the best plan can be to do nothing and stay alert, or to even meet someone in person. Be mindful in your decision-making process.

Note: Any resemblance to actual persons, living or dead, or actual events in these fictional scenarios is purely coincidental. These have been compiled simply to help you imagine how you might proceed in various situations. Names, dates, locations, and details were made up at random.

Scenario No. 1: Classified Lawyer

Paul Martin is a U.S. National Security Agency contractor at a large consulting firm with high security clearance. During the normal course of his work migrating data from one server to another, Martin sees a series of files that describe the collection of voice prints and monitoring of voice conversations of U.S.

citizens for red-flag words. Though Martin is tempted to take a screen capture or save the files, he decides not to do so. Martin is aware that the software that monitors his computer will have already logged the fact that he viewed the files.

Martin goes home at the end of the day knowing that documentation exists of the government's practice of voice-printing. All he has is the knowledge of its existence. He wants to reach out to a lawyer to weigh his options.

Risk Assessment

Who (adversary) doesn't want Martin to blow the whistle?

The NSA, U.S. intelligence agencies in general, the U.S. government, his consulting firm, and any firms involved in developing voice-printing technology and collection all have a vested interest in this information being kept secret.

What information (assets) does Martin have that they want?

If Martin chooses to disclose the existence of this program, his adversaries will want to know his identity and the identities of anyone he has contacted.

What methods does Martin's adversary have at their disposal and how far will they go to get the information?

All of the digital surveillance systems one can imagine could be brought against Martin. This might include analysis of logs of who accessed information pertaining to voice-printing. If he communicates with anyone and mentions "voice prints," this phrase could be a red flag, particularly because Martin is an intelligence contractor.

Additionally, at some point Martin may have to take a polygraph test to maintain his security clearance. If he is asked about disclosing information outside of protected channels, he will either have to confess or lose his clearance. If he is suspected of disclosure, surveillance could be set up to monitor his behavior and his contacts 24/7.

What are the risks? What happens if Martin's adversary succeeds?

If he discloses any information outside of protected channels and is identified, he will be at the very least retaliated against professionally and in the worst case prosecuted and jailed.

Strategy

Martin knows that if he reports internally, his information will likely go nowhere, and in the worst-case scenario, he will be retaliated against. Instead, his best option is to find a partner— ideally a lawyer with a high security clearance like his own or someone at a public advocacy organization.

Martin goes to the local library and uses Incognito mode on the library computer's browser to research lawyers and organizations that have previously represented government whistleblowers in the intelligence fields. Martin decides on one to contact and writes down the Wire username that is listed on their website. Martin closes the browser to ensure the history is deleted and leaves the library. That weekend, Martin dresses normally, but packs a hoodie and hat in his backpack. He leaves his smartphone at home but brings $200 in cash. He takes public transport and walks by foot to a store that carries cheap Android tablets. He buys one with cash while wearing his hoodie and hat. Then he travels, again by public transit, to another part of town.

Sitting in a fast-food restaurant with free Wi-Fi, Martin configures his tablet with a new email account and signs up for Wire. He messages the lawyer at the public advocacy organization, asking if they can meet in person in a park the next week. He requests that for the meeting the lawyer travels by foot and does not bring their smartphone. Martin uses "timed messages" that disappear shortly after they've been read, leaving no trace of his communication to the lawyer.

Upon meeting the lawyer in the park a few days later, Martin explains the issue in broad strokes without specifics. The two discuss his options and make a plan to stay in communication. They decide to anonymously apprise members of Congress with high security clearance of the existence of this information. The lawyer has done this in the past with success and thinks it might work well for Martin's situation.

Scenario No. 2: Government Agency Employee

Fulan AlFulani works for the United States Environmental Protection Agency in the Office of Research and Development in downtown D.C. AlFulani is enraged that his office has been unable to release an unclassified report because a new administrator of the EPA has barred its release. The report connects lack of oversight of the fracking industry to water-table pollution. AlFulani has access to a physical copy of the report. AlFulani wants the public to have access to the report, which will show that the administrator has been favoring the gas industry over the public.

Risk Assessment

Who (adversary) doesn't want AlFulani to blow the whistle?

It's a formidable list. The Office of the Administrator, the EPA, the whole of the U.S. federal government, and potentially the entire oil industry all have an interest in the report not becoming public.

What information (assets) does AlFulani have that they want?

AlFulani's assets include his identity and a physical copy of the report.

What methods does AlFulani's adversary have at their disposal and how far will they go to get the information?

AlFulani can assume that all work computers and digital access to files or emails can be tracked by the EPA. If a case were ever brought against AlFulani, his personal digital records and computers could be subpoenaed.

What are the risks? What happens if AlFulani's adversary succeeds?

If AlFulani is discovered to have disclosed this information, it is probable that he will suffer professional retaliation. He will lose his job or at least be ineligible for future promotion. After working at the EPA and within the federal government for more than ten years, he would have a hard time getting another job.

Strategy

AlFulani knows that all digital devices at work should be thought of as compromised. He decides to take steps to release the information anonymously.

AlFulani leaves his smartphone at home and uses public transportation to go to an electronics store in another part of D.C. He purchases a small Android tablet and a $20 prepaid Visa gift card using cash. He then goes to a coffee shop where he hasn't been before, and connects the tablet to the Wi-Fi. He creates a pseudonymous email address to register the tablet. AlFulani creates and memorizes a long passphrase to unlock the device, then turns on disk encryption in the settings. AlFulani downloads two applications: Orbot and Tor Browser, so that he can connect to Tor and do research anonymously.

Using Tor, he searches for journalists who have covered the EPA and the fracking industry, as well as organizations in D.C. that work with whistleblowers on climate change. He finds one organization, but they offer only office phone numbers, email addresses, or web forms to communicate with whistleblowers. Knowing that none of these options are secure, AlFulani skips reaching out to this organization. He soon finds the journalist Jan Jansen, who has covered fracking and the EPA previously. Jansen lists a ProtonMail address on his publication's website.

Using Tor, AlFulani signs up for a ProtonMail account, paying for it with the prepaid Visa gift card that he purchased in cash earlier. He chooses another pseudonym for this account name and memorizes the passphrase. He sends Jansen a simple first contact email, including a request to switch to Wire. Before sending the email, AlFulani downloads Wire and sets up a new account.

At this point, AlFulani must be patient and never use his tablet or even leave it turned on at home, work, or any place that he routinely frequents. Every other morning before work, AlFulani walks to a different coffee shop, turns on the tablet, and uses the public Wi-Fi to connect to the internet. He checks Wire and ProtonMail. He is careful not to do this around his workplace, but gets off the train in a different location each day. After a week, Jansen responds via Wire.

AlFulani and Jansen decide on two times during the week that they will both be available on Wire to communicate. AlFulani always uses his pseudonym. AlFulani uses his tablet to take a photo of the report as a sample and sends it to Jansen over Wire, using "timed messages," so that the image disappears after a day. This gives Jansen enough of a glimpse to see that AlFulani has the information he claims to have.

Once Jansen commits to never hand the report back to the EPA for verification or publish unsanitized versions of the report (which could lead to AlFulani's identification), the two decide where AlFulani will leave the physical report for Jansen.

Finally, after AlFulani has given Jansen all the information, AlFulani buys a new tablet, signs up for a new ProtonMail account and a new Wire account, and deletes the old accounts. He takes the old tablet and resets it, destroys it, and throws it out in a random location. The two continue weekly check-ins.

Scenario No. 3: Talking to the Press After Being Harassed

Marie Nováková works at a PR agency and has been sexually harassed. She has confirmed that a number of her colleagues have been harassed as well. Because the harasser is a prominent figure in the company, Nováková does not feel comfortable going within the company to HR. While she has talked to a lawyer, she thinks it is time for the public to be informed about the systemic issues at the company.

In this scenario, the information that Nováková needs to defend is her identity and the identities of her coworkers. Nováková first needs to find a journalist with whom she can work. On a computer at home or somewhere outside of work, she reads articles by journalists who have covered these types of stories before to find a journalist who has covered sexual harassment in her industry.

Risk Assessment

Who (adversary) doesn't want Nováková to blow the whistle?

Her harasser and her company have a vested interest in avoiding bad publicity. Clients of the firm may also have an interest in this, since it could potentially reflect poorly on them, and their interactions with the harasser might also be scrutinized. If the company has shareholders or other investors, they too would oppose any publicity that might hurt the value of their holdings.

What information (assets) does Nováková have that they want?

Nováková has her own story and a list of colleagues who will support her. She also has text messages from her harasser, substantiating portions of her allegations.

What methods does Nováková's adversary have at their disposal and how far will they go to get the information?

As a PR company, the firm is familiar with how to spin a story, and is ready to put in place a smear campaign against Nováková and those aligned with her. The firm can also retaliate against her and make life difficult at work. Finally, they may attempt to have someone remove the text messages from her phone.

What are the risks? What happens if Nováková's adversary succeeds?

Nováková could end up in court for years if the company tries to sue her over an unrelated issue, such as taking company property. She could be fired. She may be isolated from her coworkers and labeled a "troublemaker." She may have trouble getting work in the same field again.

Strategy

Nováková would like to take her story and her colleagues' stories to the press. At home or at a library (not at work), Nováková does research on which journalists and media outlets have covered her company, industry, and clients. She also looks into journalists who have previously written in support of victims of sexual harassment and assault.

She talks to her lawyer about the potential legal ramifications of sharing her story. They suggest a number of trustworthy journalists who have worked with the law firm. After creating a handwritten list of possible journalists to contact, Nováková and her lawyer agree on one who might be the right option.

The lawyer reaches out to this journalist directly and asks to have a meeting, not disclosing Nováková's name over the phone or in email. Once the journalist agrees to meet, the three meet in person and work together on a strategy for how to cover Nováková's story.

Nováková never discusses any of this at her job, and only talks to her colleagues about their stories when they're off work premises and not during work hours. She gives her lawyer a list of people who could corroborate her account and possibly add their own stories. She also backs up her phone data, including her text messages, and puts it all on a USB stick, which she gives to her lawyer for safekeeping.

Scenario No. 4: Getting Documentation Out of the Country

Fulano de Tal is a college student in Venezuela. The country is currently in flux amid mass protests against economic policies and alleged human-rights abuses by the government. The student has been joining protests and was filming them with his phone. He captured pro-government forces executing a protester. Thankfully, de Tal got away from the protest without being stopped, but he is afraid that he was seen filming. He intends to post the video anonymously online.

Risk Assessment
Who (adversary) doesn't want de Tal to blow the whistle?

The government, pro-government forces, and the specific individuals who were involved in the execution of the protester all have a vested interest in keeping de Tal's video and any allegations that he might share out of the public eye. Anyone who witnessed de Tal filming and could identify him is a potential adversary in this scenario, including bystanders who might be forced to talk, are also potential adversaries.

What information (assets) does de Tal have that they want?

Assets include the video, any copies of the video, de Tal's phone, and his memory of the event.

What methods does de Tal's adversary have at their disposal and how far will they go to get the information?

They may be monitoring all internet traffic in and out of the country. The pro-government forces can question any protestors, and even compel them to talk. De Tal and any observers may even be in physical danger.

What are the risks? What happens if de Tal's adversary succeeds?

His life is at risk, as are the lives of those he knows, in addition to any bystanders who might be able to identify him.

Strategy

Not being very good with technology, de Tal goes to a close friend's home. His friend is good with technology and has a computer. The two use a VPN to mask their IP address, knowing that Tor might be unreliable, blocked, or a red flag. Using Incognito mode in their browser, they download MAT2, a metadata removal program, and use it to remove all metadata from the video. They subsequently delete the video from de Tal's phone, put a backup copy of the video on an encrypted USB stick, and hide it.

The two choose to upload the video anonymously to Riseup. net, which has an anonymous hosting service for files. These files remain live for a week. They choose this as the file host rather than YouTube, Facebook, or other large hosts because a file can be anonymously uploaded to Riseup.net, and it will be less likely to be taken down (the video contains graphic violence, so might violate the terms of service of other hosts). After uploading the video, the two save the unique link to the hosted video, https://share.riseup. net/#aRoVbuEapdna7MYk7zjhDQ. They open a new Yahoo! Mail account, then send an email to 10 journalists at major newspapers with a link to the video and an explanation. They memorize the email account's log-in details and delete their browser history. They then delete this video file from the computer, and reset de Tal's phone, effectively deleting any history of the video's creation.

The two discuss the pros and cons of leaving town—and the country—versus simply lying low.

Recommendations for Partners

Whether you are a lawyer, journalist, public servant, member of a public advocacy organization, or simply someone who wants to help those who are trying to disclose fraud, abuse, harassment, or other unethical practices, you must make an effort to stay up to date and informed on the best practices for digital privacy and security. As you are surely aware, the world is digital, and becoming a Luddite is not an option if you are going to work with and support others, so make an effort to learn *now*. If you wait, it will only get harder.

Start by practicing with the tools and techniques listed in this book. Install the tools listed here and go practice with them in a low-stakes way. If you don't use software daily, it will be hard to avoid mistakes when it's real and the stakes are high. Get on Tor and do research anonymously. The only way to feel comfortable is to practice. If you aren't familiar with these tools, how can you expect those who reach out to you to be confident in working with you?

Go install Signal right now. Go install Wire right now. Try them out!

Another great way to learn is to take a training course on digital privacy and security tools. Lots of organizations out there provide such training courses, but take a look at what the Digital Security

Exchange, the Electronic Frontier Foundation, the Freedom of the Press Foundation, and Tactical Tech offer. See who they link to for other resources.

Once you've practiced communicating securely, you need to make sure you publicly announce safe ways that disclosers can get in contact with you:

- List your messenger account names on your organization's website.
- If you have your own website, list your messenger account names there as well.
- Update your social accounts to list your preferred method for initial secure communication and list that account name (Signal or Wire).
- Create a Keybase account and verify the ownership of your website, your email accounts, and your social accounts such as Twitter and LinkedIn.

By listing these accounts on Keybase or your organization's website, you can set out a welcome mat to potential disclosers, demonstrating that you take privacy and security seriously and that you want them to be able to trust that you are who you say you are, not a honeypot.

If you want to keep your work and personal life a bit more separate, get a different phone. Install Signal on that phone. You can practice compartmentalization, too. You will likely feel more comfortable sharing the phone number of this secure phone publicly than you would your own personal phone. This is good, because you will need to list a phone number for Signal. Register Wire with your work email address or a ProtonMail email address that you've created to talk with disclosers.

Stay logged in to your messenger accounts and get into the habit of checking them daily. If you don't see a message come in, then how can you respond? The initial response time when someone reaches out can make or break someone's willingness to work with you. In the case of John Doe initially reaching out to Bastian Obermayer, prior to the Panama Papers disclosure, Obermayer responded quickly on a messaging platform. That probably made Doe feel more comfortable about moving forward.

Once you start talking with someone, be open and discuss the best ways of working together. Don't force them into a single way of working. Discuss the pros and cons and explain to them why you like to work a certain way. Openness in discussing privacy and security will help show that you take them seriously. Be upfront about what you don't know. Be open to learning more and talking about it.

Do a risk assessment together. Think through who your adversaries are and what they might want, and list (and if possible, increase) your capabilities and decrease your vulnerabilities. While doing this, always create backup plans for communicating and reauthenticating with each other. This will not only help you both create a safe plan for working together, but will also strengthen your relationship by creating trust.

Trust takes time. Be upfront about your expectations. Create timelines and stick to them. By setting and meeting expectations, you can work toward a stronger relationship that will be more resilient to the challenges that will be thrown your way.

Finally, consider your ethical responsibility to the person on the other end. Perhaps this process is too dangerous for them, and they should reconsider disclosing the information. Should you counsel them to talk to a different partner instead of you? By investing in fair and ethical practices with everyone with whom you work, you will get farther and sleep better at night.

Just as you should learn more about digital security tools and techniques, you must stay up-to-date on applicable laws. If you aren't a lawyer or don't know the current legal status around working with a discloser in your particular situation, consult a lawyer or organization that does.

If you happen to get something anonymous in the mail, do not scan it and put it online. Consult a security expert to decide the best way to handle it. As we've seen, those who try to disclose by sending anonymous materials often aren't aware of sanitization best practices and likely have left some piece of identifying information in the materials that they provide. Do not post online any of the ancillary material around the document, like the box it came in or any identifying material. Destroy it. Instead of publishing a document directly online, consider scanning it and redacting sensitive portions using PDF Redact Tools. This will convert it to a black-and-white format and help remove microdots.[222] Even better, have the document transcribed to digital text and only post that.

If someone questions the veracity of a document, you can show it to select individuals, but carefully consider this before taking an action such as sending the document back to its point of origin for confirmation of its authenticity. By releasing this material, you could very easily point the finger directly at the discloser, or at yourself. It is likely in everyone's best interest for you to make use of the material as background to your efforts, but not to release it. Of course, be aware that even requesting the same documents from the government through legitimate means can inadvertently point to your source, as was the case with Terry J. Albury, who disclosed material to *The Intercept*.[223]

Be a proponent of safe digital techniques within your organization and proselytize to your colleagues. If you are in a position of power within your organization, make training your staff to safely use digital tools and techniques a priority. Appoint someone within your organization to lead this digital safety initiative. While some changes can come from the bottom up, establishing digital safety as a priority within your organization from the top can go a long way.

Do a security audit of your organization and any related websites. Be sure to get rid of web contact forms. They generally aren't secure, and they instead convey to the world that you don't take the security of potential whistleblowers seriously. Instead, set up secure anonymous ways of letting people reach out to you, such as SecureDrop.

Work on making your environment a safe space for those internal to your organization and those with whom you partner. Work on being a good bystander. Listen to others and watch out for those who are abusing power.

Good luck and be mindful in your choices. They will have long-lasting effects.

Appendix

Social Contract

In writing this book, I have sought to provide information to others so that they can safely and anonymously disclose information. I have sought to overcome my biases and endeavored to be a reliable source.

The reader needs to be able to rely on the information provided in this book, and know that if it is followed, it will not compromise their livelihood or well-being. The following is a social contract that is derived from the Tails Social Contract, which, in turn, was derived from the social contracts of Tor and Debian (the operating system that Tails is based on).

Here is my commitment to you, the reader.

1) In writing this book, I have tried to provide usable information on tools, techniques, and systems allowing the reader to be anonymous, private, and secure.

I believe that privacy, the free exchange of ideas, and equal access to information are essential to free and open societies. Through the techniques and the best practices that this book describes, you will be empowered to protect and advance these ideals.

2) Open and transparent information is a key to success.

When possible, all reasoning for what is written has been included, and references have been linked for further explanation.

3) I will never intentionally harm you, the reader.

The information provided is the most accurate information at the time of writing. I will never willingly include false or misleading information, and am upfront about the known issues with the tools, techniques, and best practices included.

4) The reader is given the means to decide how much they can rely on the information provided.

Readers should inform themselves and decide whether the tools and techniques included here are suitable for their use and how much they can trust the information provided.

Please do more research and consult third-party documentation and other opinions to make informed decisions. Empower yourself to learn about the tools and techniques covered in this book.

Organizations for Legal and Digital Support

CryptoParty

https://www.cryptoparty.in

This is a decentralized network of local groups who host events to train participants in the use of privacy and security technology.

Digital Security Exchange

https://dsx.us/

Digital Security Exchange connects organizations in need of digital security training with trainers.

Electronic Frontier Foundation

https://www.eff.org/

This nonprofit organization in the United States defends civil liberties in the digital world through litigation, community activism, and technology development.

ExposeFacts

https://exposefacts.org/

This U.S.–based organization combines reporting and legal advice for whistleblowers under one umbrella.

Freedom of the Press Foundation

https://freedom.press/

This U.S.–based organization supports public-interest journalism, provides digital security training and materials, and maintains the SecureDrop system.

Government Accountability Project

https://www.whistleblower.org/

Despite the name, GAP is not strictly focused on government reforms. It also works with corporate and government whistleblowers in the United States and advocates strongly for whistleblower protections worldwide.

Open Democracy Advice Centre

http://www.opendemocracy.org.za/

This nonprofit in South Africa supports whistleblowers and individuals focused on transparency.

Project on Government Oversight

http://pogo.org/

POGO is a nonpartisan independent watchdog that works with whistleblowers on reforms in the United States government.

Protect

https://www.protect-advice.org.uk/

Protect supports and advocates for whistleblowers in the U.K.

Public Employees for Environmental Responsibility

https://www.peer.org/

The nonprofit focuses on environmental issues and supporting U.S. government whistleblowers.

The Signals Network

https://thesignalsnetwork.org

The Signals Network is a relatively new organization that supports the intersection of whistleblowing and journalism.

APPENDIX

Tactical Technology Collective

https://tacticaltech.org/

This nonprofit collective in Germany provides digital security guidance and training.

Transparency International

https://www.transparency.org/

Transparency International is a global whistleblower advocacy organization with more than 100 national chapters around the world and headquarters in Berlin.

Whistleblower Aid

https://whistlebloweraid.org/

This is a relatively new legal group focused on government whistleblowers in the U.S., employing high security standards, and using proper legal channels for disclosure.

Whistleblowing International Network

https://whistleblowingnetwork.org/

WIN is an emerging global coalition of organizations with experience advising and protecting whistleblowers.

Whistleblower Netzwerk E.V.

https://www.whistleblower-net.de

This is a whistleblower support organization in Germany.

Women's Law Center's The Legal Network for Gender Equity

https://nwlc.org/about/nwlc-legal-network/

This legal support organization in the United States focuses on sexual harassment and other forms of sex and gender discrimination.

Endnotes

1   Jones, James H. *Bad Blood: The Tuskegee Syphilis Experiment*. New and Expanded ed. New York: Toronto: New York: Free Press; Maxwell Macmillan Canada; Maxwell MacMillan International, 1993.

2   Jones, James H. *Bad Blood: The Tuskegee Syphilis Experiment*. New and Expanded ed. New York: Toronto: New York: Free Press; Maxwell Macmillan Canada; Maxwell MacMillan International, 1993.

3   Heller, Jean. "Syphilis Victims in U.S. Study Went Untreated for 40 Years." *New York Times*, July 26, 1972.

4   "Tuskegee Study - Presidential Apology - CDC - NCHHSTP." https://www.cdc.gov/tuskegee/clintonp.htm.

5   "Tuskegee Study - Research Implications - CDC - NCHHSTP." https://www.cdc.gov/tuskegee/after.htm.

6   Griffin, Riley, Hannah Recht, and Jeff Green. "#MeToo's First Year Ends With More Than 425 Accused." Bloomberg. October 5, 2018. https://www.bloomberg.com/graphics/2018-me-too-anniversary/.

7   "#MeToo And The Law." NPR. April 28, 2018. https://www.npr.org/2018/04/28/606716555/-metoo-and-the-law.

8   Farrow, Ronan. "Behind the Scenes of Harvey Weinstein's Arrest." May 24, 2018. https://www.newyorker.com/news/news-desk/behind-the-scenes-of-harvey-weinsteins-impending-arrest.

9   Steinmetz, Katy. "The Edward Snowden Name Game: Whistle-Blower, Traitor, Leaker." *Time*. July 10, 2013. http://newsfeed.time.com/2013/07/10/the-edward-snowden-name-game-whistle-blower-traitor-leaker/.

10   Kent, Tom. "Whistle-Blower or Leaker?," June 10, 2013. https://web.archive.org/web/20130717084438/http://blog.ap.org/2013/06/10/whistle-blower-or-leaker/.

11   "Word Watch: Whistleblower | On The Media." WNYC. February 13, 2015. https://www.wnyc.org/story/word-watch-whistleblower/.

12 "Directive of the European Parliament and of The Council on the Protection of Persons Reporting on Breaches of Union Law," April 23, 2018. https://ec.europa.eu/info/law/better-regulation/initiatives/com-2018-218_en.

13 Osterhaus, Anja, Craig Fagan, and Transparency International. "Alternative to Silence: Whistleblower Protection in 10 European Countries." Berlin: Transparency International. 2009. https://www.transparency.org/whatwedo/publication/alternative_to_silence_whistleblower_protection_in_10_european_countries.

14 Worth, Mark. "Whistleblowing in Europe Legal Protections for Whistleblowers in the EU." Berlin: Transparency International. 2013. https://www.transparency.org/whatwedo/publication/whistleblowing_in_europe_legal_protections_for_whistleblowers_in_the_eu.

15 "Transparency International - True Stories - School Sting." https://www.transparency.org/news/story/school_sting.

16 Aranha, Jovita. "UN Prize Winning Anti-Corruption Platform Records Bribery Cases Worth Rs 2875 Cr!" *The Better India*, January 22, 2018. https://www.thebetterindia.com/124251/anti-corruption-un-award/.

17 Rauhofer, Judith. "Blowing the Whistle on Sarbanes-Oxley: Anonymous Hotlines and the Historical Stigma of Denunciation in Modern Germany." *International Review Of Law Computers & Technology* 21, no. 3 (November 2007): 363–76. http://dx.doi.org/10.1080/13600860701714507.

18 Müller-Enbergs, Helmut, ed. Inoffizielle Mitarbeiter des Ministeriums für Staatssicherheit, 3rd edn. Links Verlag, Berlin, 1996.

19 Woodford, Michael. "Whistle-Blower Stands with 'Nail That Sticks up' in Kake Scandal." The Asahi Shimbun, July 3, 2017, sec. Point of View. https://web.archive.org/web/20180907155757/http://www.asahi.com/ajw/articles/AJ201707030016.html.

20 Woodford, Michael. *Exposure: Inside the Olympus Scandal: How I Went from CEO to Whistleblower.* Reprint edition. Portfolio, 2014.

21 Bloxham, Eleanor. "What U.S. Companies Can Learn from Olympus." *Fortune*, January 26, 2012. https://fortune.com/2012/01/26/what-u-s-companies-can-learn-from-olympus/.

22 Clarke, Thomas. *International Corporate Governance: A Comparative Approach.* 2nd ed. New York: Routledge, 2017.

23 Association of Certified Fraud Examiners. "2016 ACFE Report to the Nations." http://www.acfe.com/rttn2016/docs/2016-report-to-the-nations.pdf.

24   Devine, Tom, and Tarek F. Maassarani. *The Corporate Whistleblower's Survival Guide: A Handbook for Committing the Truth*. San Francisco: Berrett-Koehler Publishers, 2011.

25   Schwartz, Ephraim. "Support Your Local Whistle-Blower." InfoWorld, June 20, 2006. https://www.infoworld.com/article/2657264/security/support-your-local-whistle-blower.html.

26   Evans, Robert, and Linda Almonte. "5 Terrible Things I Learned as a Corporate Whistleblower." Cracked, April 7, 2014. https://www.cracked.com/personal-experiences-1312-5-terrible-things-i-learned-as-corporate-whistleblower.html.

27   Pressley, George. "Linda Almonte's Whistleblower Submission to SEC," October 30, 2010. https://www.scribd.com/document/45546777/Almonte-SEC-Letter.

28   Berlin, Loren. "JPMorgan Chase Whistleblower: 'Essentially Suicide' To Stand Up To Bank." HuffPost, May 7, 2012. https://www.huffpost.com/entry/linda-almonte-jpmorgan-chase-whistleblower_n_1478268.

29   Ethics & Compliance Initiative. "Global Business Ethics Survey: The State of Ethics and Compliance in the Workplace." https://www.ethics.org/knowledge-center/2018-gbes/.

30   Robinson, Matt, and Faux Zeke. "What Happened When Elon Musk Set Out to Destroy a Junior Engineer." Bloomberg, March 13, 2019. https://www.bloomberg.com/news/features/2019-03-13/when-elon-musk-tried-to-destroy-tesla-whistleblower-martin-tripp.

31   Hull, Dana, and Jef Felley. "Tesla's Alleged Saboteur Sued by Carmaker Over Data Theft." Bloomberg, June 20, 2018. https://www.bloomberg.com/news/articles/2018-06-20/tesla-sues-former-employee-for-allegedly-hacking-trade-secrets.

32   Lopez, Linette. "Internal Documents Reveal Tesla Is Blowing through an Insane Amount of Raw Material and Cash to Make Model 3s, and Production Is Still a Nightmare." *Business Insider*, June 4, 2018. https://www.businessinsider.com/tesla-model-3-scrap-waste-high-gigafactory-2018-5.

33   Feldblum, Chai R., and Victoria A. Lipnic. "Select Task Force on the Study of Harassment in the Workplace." U.S. Equal Employment Opportunity Commission, June 2016. https://www.eeoc.gov/eeoc/task_force/harassment/upload/report.pdf.

34   Johnson, Stefanie K., Jessica Kirk, and Ksenia Keplinger. "Why We Fail to Report Sexual Harassment." *Harvard Business Review*, October 4, 2016. https://hbr.org/2016/10/why-we-fail-to-report-sexual-harassment.

35   Cortina, Lilia M., and Jennifer L. Berdahl. "Sexual Harassment in Organizations: A Decade of Research in Review." In The SAGE Handbook of Organizational Behavior: Volume I - Micro Approaches, 469–97. United Kingdom: SAGE Publications Ltd, 2008. https://doi.org/10.4135/9781849200448.n26.

36   Johnson, Stefanie K., Jessica Kirk, and Ksenia Keplinger. "Why We Fail to Report Sexual Harassment." Harvard Business Review, October 4, 2016. https://hbr.org/2016/10/why-we-fail-to-report-sexual-harassment.

37   Benner, Katie. "Women in Tech Speak Frankly on Culture of Harassment." New York Times, June 30, 2017, sec. Technology. https://www.nytimes.com/2017/06/30/technology/women-entrepreneurs-speak-out-sexual-harassment.html.

38   Ransohoff, Sarah. "Things a Startup Has Instead of H.R." The New Yorker, February 18, 2018. https://www.newyorker.com/humor/daily-shouts/things-a-startup-has-instead-of-hr.

39   Johnson, Stefanie K., Jessica Kirk, and Ksenia Keplinger. "Why We Fail to Report Sexual Harassment." Harvard Business Review, October 4, 2016. https://hbr.org/2016/10/why-we-fail-to-report-sexual-harassment.

40   Miller, Claire Cain. "It's Not Just Fox: Why Women Don't Report Sexual Harassment." New York Times, December 22, 2017, sec. The Upshot. https://www.nytimes.com/2017/04/10/upshot/its-not-just-fox-why-women-dont-report-sexual-harassment.html.

41   Johnson, W. Brad, and David G. Smith. "Too Many Men Are Silent Bystanders to Sexual Harassment." Harvard Business Review, March 13, 2017. https://hbr.org/2017/03/too-many-men-are-silent-bystanders-to-sexual-harassment.

42   Byers, Dylan. "21st Century Fox Stands by Bill O'Reilly amid Report of Five Settlements." CNNMoney, April 1, 2017. https://money.cnn.com/2017/04/01/media/bill-oreilly-settlements/index.html.

43   Vogel, Pam. "The Infrastructure That Enabled Serial Sexual Harassment at Fox Is Still Working." Salon, October 28, 2017. https://www.salon.com/2017/10/28/the-infrastructure-that-enabled-serial-sexual-harassment-at-fox-is-still-working_partner/.

44   Civil Rights Act of 1964 § 7, 42 U.S.C. § 2000e et seq (1964). https://www.eeoc.gov/laws/statutes/titlevii.cfm.

45   "Preventing Gender-Based Workplace Discrimination and Harassment: New Data on 193 Countries." WORLD Policy Analysis Center, 2017. https://www.worldpolicycenter.org/sites/default/files/WORLD%20Discrimination%20at%20Work%20Report.pdf

46   Pozen, David E. "The Leaky Leviathan: Why the Government Condemns and Condones Unlawful Disclosures of Information." *Harvard Law Review* 127, no. 2 (2013): 512–635. http://www.jstor.org/stable/23742018.

47   Parker, Ashley, and David Nakamura. "In Tweet Storm, Trump Decries 'Illegal Leaks' and Asserts 'All Agree' He Has Complete Power to Pardon." *Washington Post*, July 22, 2017, sec. Politics. https://www.washingtonpost.com/news/post-politics/wp/2017/07/22/trump-denounces-illegal-leaks-in-new-accounts-of-his-campaigns-contact-with-russia/.

48   Obama, Barack. "Transparency and Open Government." Memorandum for the Heads of Executive Departments and Agencies, January 21, 2009. https://obamawhitehouse.archives.gov/the-press-office/transparency-and-open-government.

49   The Obama-Biden Transition Team. "Ethics | Change.Gov," September 21, 2016. https://web.archive.org/web/20160921064304/http://change.gov/agenda/ethics_agenda/.

50   McVeigh, Karen. "Obama's Efforts to Control Leaks 'the Most Aggressive since Nixon', Report Finds." *The Guardian*, October 10, 2013, sec. US News. https://www.theguardian.com/world/2013/oct/10/obama-leaks-aggressive-nixon-report-prosecution.

51   Downie Jr., Leonard, and Sara Rafsky. "The Obama Administration and the Press." Committee to Protect Journalists, October 2013. https://cpj.org/reports/2013/10/obama-and-the-press-us-leaks-surveillance-post-911.php.

52   Obama, Barack. "Executive Order 13587 -- Structural Reforms to Improve the Security of Classified Networks and the Responsible Sharing and Safeguarding of Classified Information," October 7, 2011. https://obamawhitehouse.archives.gov/the-press-office/2011/10/07/executive-order-13587-structural-reforms-improve-security-classified-net.

53   "Student Guide: Insider Threat Awareness." Center for Development of Security Excellence, September 2017. https://www.dni.gov/index.php/ncsc-how-we-work/ncsc-nittf/ncsc-nittf-resource-library.

54   Radack, Jesselyn, and Kathleen McClellan. "Insider Threat Program Training and Trump's War on Leaks: A Chilling Combination for Whistleblowers." ExposeFacts, October 16, 2017. https://exposefacts.org/insider-threat-program-training-and-trumps-war-on-leaks-a-chilling-combination-for-whistleblowers/.

55   Kohn, Stephen M. "Were James Comey's Leaks Lawful?" *Washington Post*, June 8, 2017, sec. Analysis. https://www.washingtonpost.com/posteverything/wp/2017/06/08/were-james-comeys-leaks-lawful/.

56   Sterne, Peter. "Obama Used the Espionage Act to Put a Record Number of Reporters' Sources in Jail, and Trump Could Be Even Worse." Freedom of the Press Foundation, June 21, 2017. https://freedom.press/news/obama-used-espionage-act-put-record-number-reporters-sources-jail-and-trump-could-be-even-worse/.

57   Rottman, Gabe. "On Leak Prosecutions, Obama Takes It to 11. (Or Should We Say 526?)." American Civil Liberties Union, October 11, 2014. https://www.aclu.org/blog/free-speech/employee-speech-and-whistleblowers/leak-prosecutions-obama-takes-it-11-or-should-we.

58   Greenberg, David. "The Hidden History of the Espionage Act." *Slate Magazine*, December 27, 2010. https://slate.com/news-and-politics/2010/12/the-real-purpose-of-the-espionage-act.html.

59   Ho, Solarina. "Snowden Says U.S. Not Offering Fair Trial If He Returns." Reuters, March 4, 2015. https://www.reuters.com/article/us-russia-usa-snowden-idUSKBN0M023E20150304.

60   McCarthy, Tom. "Edward Snowden: 'If I Could Go Anywhere That Place Would Be Home.'" *The Guardian*, May 29, 2014, sec. World news. https://www.theguardian.com/world/2014/may/29/edward-snowden-interview-breaking-law-was-only-option-says-whistleblower.

61   Ellsberg, Daniel. "Daniel Ellsberg: Snowden Would Not Get a Fair Trial – and Kerry Is Wrong." *The Guardian*, May 30, 2014, sec. Opinion. https://www.theguardian.com/commentisfree/2014/may/30/daniel-ellsberg-snowden-fair-trial-kerry-espionage-act.

62   Maass, Peter. "Destroyed by the Espionage Act: Stephen Kim Spoke to a Reporter. Now He's in Jail. This Is His Story." *The Intercept*, February 18, 2015. https://theintercept.com/2015/02/18/destroyed-by-the-espionage-act/.

63   LaFraniere, Sharon. "Paul Manafort, Trump's Former Campaign Chairman, Guilty of 8 Counts." *New York Times*, August 21, 2018, sec. U.S. https://www.nytimes.com/2018/08/21/us/politics/paul-manafort-trial-verdict.html.

64   Mettler, Katie. "Judge Denies Bail for Accused NSA Leaker Reality Winner after Not Guilty Plea." *Washington Post*, June 9, 2017, sec. Morning Mix. https://www.washingtonpost.com/news/morning-mix/wp/2017/06/09/judges-denies-bail-for-accused-nsa-leaker-reality-winner-after-not-guilty-plea/.

65   Andone, Dakin, and Sal Sendik. "NSA Leaker Reality Winner Sentenced to More than 5 Years in Prison." CNN, August 23, 2018. https://www.cnn.com/2018/08/23/politics/reality-winner-nsa-leaker-sentenced/.

ENDNOTES

66   Maass, Peter. "Reality Winner Has Been in Jail for a Year. Her Prosecution Is Unfair and Unprecedented." *The Intercept*, June 3, 2018. https://theintercept.com/2018/06/03/reality-winner-nsa-paul-manafort/.

67   Weiner, Rachel, and Ellen Nakashima. "Chelsea Manning Subpoenaed to Testify before Grand Jury in Assange Investigation." *Washington Post*, March 1, 2019, sec. National Security. https://www.washingtonpost.com/world/national-security/chelsea-manning-subpoenaed-to-testify-before-grand-jury-in-assange-investigation/2019/03/01/fe3bd582-3c32-11e9-a06c-3ec8ed509d15_story.html.

68   Horwitz, Sari. "Julian Assange Unlikely to Face U.S. Charges over Publishing Classified Documents." *Washington Post*, November 25, 2013, sec. National Security. https://www.washingtonpost.com/world/national-security/julian-assange-unlikely-to-face-us-charges-over-publishing-classified-documents/2013/11/25/dd27decc-55f1-11e3-8304-caf30787c0a9_story.html.

69   "Whistleblower Protections: A Guide." The International Bar Association, April 2018. https://www.ibanet.org/Document/Default.aspx?DocumentUid=a8bac0a9-ea7e-472d-a48e-ee76cb3cdef8.

70   Fröhlich, Silja. "Africa 'needs to Catch up' with Protection for Whistleblowers." DW.COM, March 9, 2017. https://www.dw.com/en/africa-needs-to-catch-up-with-protection-for-whistleblowers/a-37873356.

71   Worth, Mark, Suelette Dreyfus, and Garreth Hanley. "Gaps in the System: Whistleblower Laws in the EU." Blueprint for Free Speech, 2018. https://blueprintforfreespeech.net/wp-content/uploads/2018/03/BLUEPRINT-Gaps-in-the-System-Whistleblowers-Laws-in-the-EU.pdf.

72   Worth, Mark. "Whistleblowing in Europe: Legal Protections for Whistleblowers in the EU." Transparency International, 2013. https://www.transparency.org/whatwedo/publication/whistleblowing_in_europe_legal_protections_for_whistleblowers_in_the_eu.

73   "Press Release: European Union Reaches Agreement On Historic Whistleblower Directive." Government Accountability Project, March 12, 2019. https://www.whistleblower.org/press-release/press-release-european-union-reaches-agreement-on-historic-whistleblower-directive/.

74   "Directive of the European Parliament and of The Council on the Protection of Persons Reporting on Breaches of Union Law," April 23, 2018. https://ec.europa.eu/info/law/better-regulation/initiatives/com-2018-218_en.

75   "U.N. Issues Groundbreaking Whistleblower Policy." Government Accountability Project, December 20, 2005. https://www.whistleblower.org/press/un-issues-groundbreaking-whistleblower-policy/.

76   "Representative Cases in Which the United Nations or Its Funds, Programmes
      or Agencies Have Not Complied with Best Practices in Whistleblower
      Protection." Government Accountability Project, August 2014. https://
      www.whistleblower.org/wp-content/uploads/2018/12/Representative-
      UN-Cases.pdf.

77   Whistleblower Protection Act of 1989, 5 U.S.C. § 2302(b)(8). https://www.
      govinfo.gov/content/pkg/STATUTE-103/pdf/STATUTE-103-Pg16.pdf.

78   Whistleblower Protection Enhancement Act of 2012. https://www.govinfo.
      gov/content/pkg/CRPT-112srpt155/pdf/CRPT-112srpt155.pdf.

79   10 U.S.C. § 2409; 41 U.S.C. § 4712.

80   Tiku, Nitasha. "Tech Workers Unite to Fight Forced Arbitration." *Wired*,
      January 14, 2019. https://www.wired.com/story/tech-workers-unite-fight-
      forced-arbitration/.

81   Feuer, Alan. "What We Know About Trump's $130,000 Payment to Stormy
      Daniels." *New York Times*, August 27, 2018, sec. New York. https://www.
      nytimes.com/2018/08/27/nyregion/stormy-daniels-trump-payment.
      html.

82   Whistleblower Protection Enhancement Act of 2012. https://www.govinfo.
      gov/content/pkg/CRPT-112srpt155/pdf/CRPT-112srpt155.pdf.

83   Defend Trade Secrets Act of 2016, 18 U.S.C. § 1836. https://www.congress.
      gov/bill/114th-congress/senate-bill/1890/text.

84   Weibust, Erik, Andrew Stark, and Robert A. Fisher. "Federal Court Rejects
      Defend Trade Secrets Act Whistleblower Immunity Defense on a Motion
      to Dismiss and Orders Employee to Return Stolen Trade Secrets." Trading
      Secrets, December 19, 2016. https://www.tradesecretslaw.com/2016/12/
      articles/dtsa/federal-court-rejects-defend-trade-secrets-act-whistleblower-
      immunity-defense-on-a-motion-to-dismiss-and-orders-employee-to-return-
      stolen-trade-secrets/.

85   Menell, Peter S. "Misconstruing Whistleblower Immunity Under the Defend
      Trade Secrets Act." CLS Blue Sky Blog, January 3, 2017. http://clsbluesky.law.
      columbia.edu/2017/01/03/misconstruing-whistleblower-immunity-under-
      the-defend-trade-secrets-act/.

86   Casciato, Tom, Bill Moyers, Laura Macomber, and Daniel Baer. Ag-Gag Laws
      Silence Whistleblowers, 2013. https://billmoyers.com/2013/07/10/alec-
      activists-and-ag-gag/.

87   Sledge, Matt. "Intelligence Agencies Won't Release Reports On Excessive
      Secrecy." HuffPost, January 28, 2014. https://www.huffingtonpost.
      com/2014/01/28/cia-over-classification-report_n_4680479.html.

ENDNOTES

88   Spitz, Malte. "Germans Loved Obama. Now We Don't Trust Him." *New York Times*, June 29, 2013, sec. Opinion. https://www.nytimes.com/2013/06/30/opinion/sunday/germans-loved-obama-now-we-dont-trust-him.html.

89   McCullagh, Declan, and Anne Broache. "FBI Taps Cell Phone Mic as Eavesdropping Tool." Tech News, December 1, 2006. https://web.archive.org/web/20070323052657/http://news.zdnet.com/2100-1035_22-6140191.html.

90   Snyder, Chris. "Hackers and Governments Can See You through Your Phone's Camera — Here's How to Protect Yourself." *Business Insider*, June 24, 2017. https://www.businessinsider.com/hackers-governments-smartphone-iphone-camera-wikileaks-cybersecurity-hack-privacy-webcam-2017-6.

91   Goodin, Dan. "New Exploit Turns Samsung Galaxy Phones into Remote Bugging Devices." Ars Technica, June 16, 2015. https://arstechnica.com/information-technology/2015/06/new-exploit-turns-samsung-galaxy-phones-into-remote-bugging-devices/.

92   "Panopticlick." Accessed August 26, 2019. https://panopticlick.eff.org/.

93   Sharkov, Damien. "Vladimir Putin Does Not Have a Smartphone, and He Is Proud of It." *Newsweek*, February 8, 2018. https://www.newsweek.com/why-does-vladimir-putin-avoid-smartphones-801406.

94   Dwoskin, Elizabeth, and Craig Timberg. "Google Now Knows When Its Users Go to the Store and Buy Stuff." *Washington Post*, May 23, 2017, sec. The Switch. https://www.washingtonpost.com/news/the-switch/wp/2017/05/23/google-now-knows-when-you-are-at-a-cash-register-and-how-much-you-are-spending/.

95   Valentino-DeVries, Jennifer, Natasha Singer, Michael H. Keller, and Aaron Krolik. "Your Apps Know Where You Were Last Night, and They're Not Keeping It Secret." *New York Times*, December 10, 2018, sec. Business. https://www.nytimes.com/interactive/2018/12/10/business/location-data-privacy-apps.html.

96   Hill, Kashmir. "How Target Figured Out A Teen Girl Was Pregnant Before Her Father Did." *Forbes*, February 16, 2012. https://www.forbes.com/sites/kashmirhill/2012/02/16/how-target-figured-out-a-teen-girl-was-pregnant-before-her-father-did/.

97   "Please Rob Me." Accessed August 26, 2019. http://pleaserobme.com/.

98   "I Know Where Your Cat Lives." Accessed August 27, 2019. https://iknowwhereyourcatlives.com/.

99   Slater-Robins, Max. "Using a Samsung Smart Fridge Could Leave Your Gmail Account Vulnerable to Hackers." *Business Insider*, August 24, 2015.

https://www.businessinsider.com/samsung-smart-fridge-exposes-gmail-logins-2015-8.

100 Cox, Joseph. "I Gave a Bounty Hunter $300. Then He Located Our Phone." Vice (blog), January 8, 2019. https://www.vice.com/en_us/article/nepxbz/i-gave-a-bounty-hunter-300-dollars-located-phone-microbilt-zumigo-tmobile.

101 Savage, Charlie, and Jonathan Weisman. "N.S.A. Collection of Bulk Call Data Is Ruled Illegal." New York Times, May 7, 2015, sec. U.S. https://www.nytimes.com/2015/05/08/us/nsa-phone-records-collection-ruled-illegal-by-appeals-court.html.

102 "NSA Phone Data Collection 'Not Illegal', US Court Rules." BBC News, August 28, 2015, sec. US & Canada. https://www.bbc.com/news/world-us-canada-34091702.

103 Hosenball, Mark. "NSA Collected Americans' Phone Records despite Law Change: Report." Reuters, May 2, 2017, sec. Politics. https://www.reuters.com/article/us-usa-security-surveillance-idUSKBN17Y2LS.

104 Savage, Charlie, Eileen Sullivan, and Nicholas Fandos. "House Extends Surveillance Law, Rejecting New Privacy Safeguards." New York Times, January 11, 2018, sec. U.S. https://www.nytimes.com/2018/01/11/us/politics/fisa-surveillance-congress-trump.html.

105 Nechepurenko, Ivan. "Russia Moves to Tighten Counterterror Law; Rights Activists See Threat to Freedoms." New York Times, June 24, 2016, sec. World. https://www.nytimes.com/2016/06/25/world/europe/russia-counterterrorism-yarovaya-law.html.

106 Froomkin, Dan. "How the NSA Converts Spoken Words Into Searchable Text." The Intercept, May 5, 2015. https://theintercept.com/2015/05/05/nsa-speech-recognition-snowden-searchable-text/.

107 Kofman, Ava. "Finding Your Voice: Forget About Siri and Alexa — When It Comes to Voice Identification, the 'NSA Reigns Supreme.'" The Intercept, January 19, 2018. https://theintercept.com/2018/01/19/voice-recognition-technology-nsa/.

108 "China Collecting 'Voice Pattern' Samples to Establish National Biometric Database." Human Rights Watch, October 22, 2017. https://www.hrw.org/news/2017/10/22/china-voice-biometric-collection-threatens-privacy.

109 Sudworth, John, Joyce Liu, and Wang Xiqing. "In Your Face: China's All-Seeing State," 2017. https://www.bbc.com/news/av/world-asia-china-42248056/in-your-face-china-s-all-seeing-state.

110 "Stingray Tracking Devices: Who's Got Them?" American Civil Liberties Union, October 2018. https://www.aclu.org/issues/privacy-technology/surveillance-technologies/stingray-tracking-devices-whos-got-them.

111 Harwell, Drew, and Tony Romm. "ICE Is Tapping into a Huge License-Plate Database, ACLU Says, Raising New Privacy Concerns about Surveillance." *Washington Post*, March 13, 2019, sec. Tech Policy. https://www.washingtonpost.com/technology/2019/03/13/ice-is-tapping-into-huge-license-plate-database-aclu-says-raising-new-privacy-concerns-about-surveillance/.

112 The Times Editorial Board. "Editorial: The Problem with LAPD's Predictive Policing." *Los Angeles Times*, March 16, 2019, sec. Opinion. https://www.latimes.com/opinion/editorials/la-ed-lapd-predictive-policing-20190316-story.html.

113 Greenberg, Andy. "How A 'Deviant' Philosopher Built Palantir, A CIA-Funded Data-Mining Juggernaut." *Forbes*, August 14, 2013. https://www.forbes.com/sites/andygreenberg/2013/08/14/agent-of-intelligence-how-a-deviant-philosopher-built-palantir-a-cia-funded-data-mining-juggernaut/.

114 Valentino-DeVries, Jennifer, Natasha Singer, Michael H. Keller, and Aaron Krolik. "Your Apps Know Where You Were Last Night, and They're Not Keeping It Secret." *New York Times*, December 10, 2018, sec. Business. https://www.nytimes.com/interactive/2018/12/10/business/location-data-privacy-apps.html.

115 Valentino-DeVries, Jennifer, Natasha Singer, Michael H. Keller, and Aaron Krolik. "Your Apps Know Where You Were Last Night, and They're Not Keeping It Secret." *New York Times*, December 10, 2018, sec. Business. https://www.nytimes.com/interactive/2018/12/10/business/location-data-privacy-apps.html.

116 Gallagher, Sean. "You May Already Be a Winner in NSA's 'Three-Degrees' Surveillance Sweepstakes!" Ars Technica, July 18, 2013. https://arstechnica.com/information-technology/2013/07/you-may-already-be-a-winner-in-nsas-three-degrees-surveillance-sweepstakes/.

117 "The Intercept Welcomes Whistleblowers." *The Intercept*, April 22, 2019. https://theintercept.com/source/.

118 Lee, Micah. "How to Leak to The Intercept." *The Intercept*, January 28, 2015. https://web.archive.org/web/20151124173207/https://theintercept.com/2015/01/28/how-to-leak-to-the-intercept/.

119 Hern, Alex. "Five Stupid Things Dread Pirate Roberts Did to Get Arrested." *The Guardian*, October 3, 2013, sec. Technology. https://www.theguardian.

com/technology/2013/oct/03/five-stupid-things-dread-pirate-roberts-did-to-get-arrested.

120   Lustgarten, Abrahm. "Palm Oil Was Supposed to Help Save the Planet. Instead It Unleashed a Catastrophe." *New York Times*, November 20, 2018, sec. Magazine. https://www.nytimes.com/2018/11/20/magazine/palm-oil-borneo-climate-catastrophe.html.

121   Perlberg, Steven, Chris Geidner, and Jason Leopold. "A Federal Government Contractor Has Been Charged With Leaking To The Intercept." BuzzFeed News, June 5, 2017. https://www.buzzfeednews.com/article/stevenperlberg/a-federal-government-contractor-has-been-charged-with.

122   Leetaru, Kalev. "What The 'Rogue' EPA, NPS and NASA Twitter Accounts Teach Us About The Future Of Social." *Forbes*, January 25, 2017. https://www.forbes.com/sites/kalevleetaru/2017/01/25/what-the-rogue-epa-nps-and-nasa-twitter-accounts-teach-us-about-the-future-of-social/.

123   Lee, Micah. "How to Run a Rogue Government Twitter Account With an Anonymous Email Address and a Burner Phone." *The Intercept*, February 20, 2017. https://theintercept.com/2017/02/20/how-to-run-a-rogue-government-twitter-account-with-an-anonymous-email-address-and-a-burner-phone/.

124   @thegrugq. "Twitter Activist Security." Medium, January 30, 2017. https://medium.com/@thegrugq/twitter-activist-security-7c806bae9cb0.

125   "USA v. MANAFORT et al, No. 1:17-Cr-00201-ABJ Document 315," June 4, 2018. https://www.documentcloud.org/documents/4493885-Revoke.html.

126   Scahill, Jeremy, and Josh Begley. "How Spies Stole the Keys to the Encryption Castle." *The Intercept*, February 19, 2015. https://theintercept.com/2015/02/19/great-sim-heist/.

127   "Apple's IMessage Defense Against Spying Has One Flaw." *Wired*, September 8, 2015. https://www.wired.com/2015/09/apple-fighting-privacy-imessage-still-problems/.

128   Gilbertson, Scott. "HTTPS Is Not a Magic Bullet for Web Security." Ars Technica, July 11, 2016. https://arstechnica.com/information-technology/2016/07/https-is-not-a-magic-bullet-for-web-security/.

129   "Domain Games: Role-Playing an Online Identity." Exposing the Invisible. Accessed August 26, 2019. http://exposingtheinvisible.org/resources/inspiration/domain-games.

130   Paquette, Danielle. "Lawsuit Accuses Celebrity Chef Mike Isabella of 'Extraordinary' Sexual Harassment." *Washington Post*, March 19, 2018. https://www.washingtonpost.com/business/economy/celebrity-chef-

mike-isabella-is-sued-for-extraordinary-sexual-harassment/2018/
03/19/4cc47bf4-27a4-11e8-b79d-f3d931db7f68_story.html.

131   Feldblum, Chai R., and Victoria A. Lipnic. "Select Task Force on the Study
      of Harassment in the Workplace." U.S. Equal Employment Opportunity
      Commission, June 2016. https://www.eeoc.gov/eeoc/task_force/harassment/
      upload/report.pdf.

132   "NEW YORK v. WEINSTEIN et al, NYSCEF DOC. NO. 1," February 11,
      2018. https://pmcvariety.files.wordpress.com/2018/02/ny-lg-pdf.pdf.

133   Twohey, Megan, Jodi Kantor, Susan Dominus, Jim Rutenberg, and Steve
      Eder. "Weinstein's Complicity Machine." New York Times, December 5, 2017,
      sec.   U.S.   https://www.nytimes.com/interactive/2017/12/05/us/harvey-
      weinstein-complicity.html.

134   Mitchell, Kathrine. "Kathrine Mitchell, M.D. Written Testimony." House
      Committee on Veterans Affairs, July 8, 2014. https://archives-veterans.house.
      gov/witness-testimony/kathrine-mitchell-md.

135   "Speaking Up for Science: A Guide to Whistleblowing for Federal
      Employees." Government Accountability Project, 2018. https://www.
      whistleblower.org/wp-content/uploads/2018/11/GAP_Federal-Employees-
      Whistleblower-Guide.pdf.

136   "Working with Whistleblowers: A Guide for Journalists." Government
      Accountability Project, 2017. http://www.whistleblower.org/wp-content/
      uploads/2017/11/whistleblowerguidejournalism.pdf.

137   "Inside the Mind of a Whistleblower." Ethics Resource Center, 2012. https://
      www.corporatecomplianceinsights.com/wp-content/uploads/2012/05/
      inside-the-mind-of-a-whistleblower-NBES.pdf.

138   "2018 Global Business Ethics Survey: The State of Ethics & Compliance in the
      Workplace." Ethics & Compliance Initiative, 2018. https://www.ethics.org/
      knowledge-center/2018-gbes-2/.

139   Benner, Katie. "A Nuclear Site Guard Accused Colleagues of Sexual Assault.
      Then She Was Fired." New York Times, January 25, 2019, sec. U.S. https://
      www.nytimes.com/2019/01/25/us/politics/department-of-energy-sexual-
      assault.html.

140   Glover, Jennifer. "Opinion | I Was a Nuclear Site Guard. My Colleagues
      Sexually Assaulted Me." New York Times, February 14, 2019, sec. Opinion.
      https://www.nytimes.com/2019/02/14/opinion/nuclear-site-guard-sexual-
      assault.html.

141   Lyle, Michael. "Senators Demand Answers after NYT Reports Sexual Assault
      Allegations at NNSS." Nevada Current. Accessed August 26, 2019. https://

www.nevadacurrent.com/blog/senators-demand-answers-after-nyt-reports-sexual-assault-allegations-at-nnss/.

142 Lipman, Frederick D. Whistleblowers: Incentives, Disincentives, and Protection Strategies. Wiley Corporate F&A Series. Hoboken, N.J: Wiley, 2012.

143 Cadwalladr, Carole. "'I Made Steve Bannon's Psychological Warfare Tool': Meet the Data War Whistleblower." *The Guardian*, March 18, 2018, sec. News. https://www.theguardian.com/news/2018/mar/17/data-war-whistleblower-christopher-wylie-faceook-nix-bannon-trump.

144 Cadwalladr, Carole. "Revealed: How US Billionaire Helped to Back Brexit." *The Guardian*, February 26, 2017, sec. Politics. https://www.theguardian.com/politics/2017/feb/26/us-billionaire-mercer-helped-back-brexit.

145 Fiegerman, Seth. "Mark Zuckerberg Just Finished Nearly 10 Hours of Questions from Almost 100 Lawmakers." CNNMoney, April 11, 2018. https://money.cnn.com/2018/04/11/technology/mark-zuckerberg-congress/index.html.

146 Romm, Tony, and Craig Timberg. "FTC Opens Investigation into Facebook after Cambridge Analytica Scrapes Millions of Users' Personal Information." *Washington Post*, March 20, 2018, sec. The Switch. https://www.washingtonpost.com/news/the-switch/wp/2018/03/20/ftc-opens-investigation-into-facebook-after-cambridge-analytica-scrapes-millions-of-users-personal-information/.

147 "SEC.Gov | What We Do." Accessed August 26, 2019. https://www.sec.gov/Article/whatwedo.html.

148 "Evaluation of the SEC's Whistleblower Program." Office of the Inspector General, U.S. Securities and Exchange Commissions, January 18, 2013. https://www.sec.gov/files/511.pdf.

149 DIGITAL REALTY TRUST, INC. v. SOMERS, No. 16–1276 (U.S. Supreme Court February 21, 2018).

150 Dizard, John. "Be a Whistleblower and Win a Fistful of Dollars." *Financial Times*, July 30, 2018.

151 Ranjan, Amitav. "Whistleblower Said Don't Name Me. Govt Did. He Was Shot Dead." *Indian Express*, November 29, 2003. https://web.archive.org/web/20040411223435/http://www.indianexpress.com:80/full_story.php?content_id=36329.

152 Associated Press. "Nuclear Regulatory Commission Downplays Safety Warnings, Investigation Finds." CBS News, December 20, 2017. https://www.cbsnews.com/news/nuclear-regulatory-commission-downplays-safety-warnings-investigation-finds/.

ENDNOTES

153   Zeitung, Süddeutsche. "The Manifesto of John Doe." Süddeutsche.de. Accessed February 11, 2018. http://panamapapers.sueddeutsche.de/articles/572c897a5632a39742ed34ef/.

154   "2019 World Press Freedom Index." Reporters Without Borders. Accessed August 26, 2019. https://rsf.org/en/ranking.

155   Brenner, Marie. "Jeffrey Wigand: The Man Who Knew Too Much." *Vanity Fair*, May 1996. https://www.vanityfair.com/magazine/1996/05/wigand199605.

156   Presser, Lizzie. "Safe House." *California Sunday Magazine*, October 4, 2018. https://story.californiasunday.com/safe-house.

157   "Attorney-Client Privilege in the Global Context." Ally Law, July 7, 2017. https://ally-law.com/ally-law-publishes-global-attorney-client-privilege-compendium/.

158   S.M. "Why the FBI Overrode Attorney-Client Privilege to Raid Michael Cohen's Office." *The Economist*, April 10, 2018. https://www.economist.com/democracy-in-america/2018/04/10/why-the-fbi-overrode-attorney-client-privilege-to-raid-michael-cohens-office.

159   Ackerman, Spencer, and Ewen MacAskill. "Snowden Calls for Whistleblower Shield after Claims by New Pentagon Source." *The Guardian*, May 22, 2016, sec. US news. https://www.theguardian.com/us-news/2016/may/22/snowden-whistleblower-protections-john-crane.

160   Ibrahim, Mukhtar M. "Minneapolis FBI Agent Charged with Leaking Classified Information to Reporter." MPR News, March 28, 2018. https://www.mprnews.org/story/2018/03/28/minneapolis-fbi-agent-charged-with-leaking-classified-information.

161   "Application for Search Warrant, Case 17-Mj-670 (DTS), Document 3." United States District Court for the District of Minnesota, January 2, 2018. https://www.documentcloud.org/documents/4426181-Minneapolis-FBI-Agent-Search-Warrant-Application.html.

162   Harding, Luke. *The Snowden Files: The Inside Story of the World's Most Wanted Man.* F First Paperback Edition Used edition. New York: Vintage, 2014.

163   "Freedom of the Press 2017." Freedom House, April 18, 2017. https://freedomhouse.org/report/freedom-press/freedom-press-2017.

164   "The Intercept Welcomes Whistleblowers." *The Intercept*, April 22, 2019. https://theintercept.com/source/.

165   "Directory." SecureDrop. Accessed August 26, 2019. https://securedrop.org/directory/.

166   Associated Press. "Respected Media Outlets Collaborate with WikiLeaks." Text.Article. Associated Press, March 27, 2015. https://www.foxnews.com/world/respected-media-outlets-collaborate-with-wikileaks.

167   Hansen, Evan. "Manning-Lamo Chat Logs Revealed." *Wired*, July 13, 2011. https://www.wired.com/2011/07/manning-lamo-logs/.

168   Abrams, Abigail. "Kate Upton Accuses Guess Co-Founder of 'Sexually and Emotionally' Harassing Women." *Time*, February 1, 2018. https://time.com/5129697/kate-upton-guess-paul-marciano-sexual-harassment-accusation/.

169   Stanhope, Kate. "CBS 'Looking Into' Jeremy Piven Sexual Harassment Allegations." The *Hollywood Reporter*, October 31, 2017. https://www.hollywoodreporter.com/live-feed/cbs-looking-jeremy-piven-sexual-harassment-allegations-1053510.

170   Ursu, Anne. "Sexual Harassment in the Children's Book Industry." Medium, February 8, 2018. https://medium.com/@anneursu_10179/sexual-harassment-in-the-childrens-book-industry-3417048ccde2.

171   Barsanti, Sam. "Former Community Writer Megan Ganz Calls out Dan Harmon for Misconduct." The A.V. Club, January 3, 2018. https://www.avclub.com/former-community-writer-megan-ganz-calls-out-dan-harmon-1821754073.

172   DeKort, Michael. Original-See Other Copy If This Version Is Frozen, 2006. https://www.youtube.com/watch?v=qd3VV8Za04g.

173   Helvarg, David. *Rescue Warriors: The U.S. Coast Guard, America's Forgotten Heroes*. 1 edition. New York: St. Martin's Griffin, 2010.

174   Honan, Mat. "What Is Doxing?" *Wired*, March 6, 2014. https://www.wired.com/2014/03/doxing/.

175   Horton, Scott. "The Persecution of LtCmdr Matthew Diaz." Browsings: The Harper's Blog, May 14, 2007. https://harpers.org/blog/2007/05/the-persecution-of-ltcmdr-matthew-diaz/.

176   Golden, Tim. "Naming Names at Gitmo." *New York Times*, October 21, 2007, sec. Magazine. https://www.nytimes.com/2007/10/21/magazine/21Diaz-t.html.

177   Golden, Tim. "Naming Names at Gitmo." *New York Times*, October 21, 2007, sec. Magazine. https://www.nytimes.com/2007/10/21/magazine/21Diaz-t.html.

178   Greenberg, Andy. "These Are the Emails Snowden Sent to First Introduce His Epic NSA Leaks." *Wired*, October 13, 2014. https://www.wired.com/2014/10/snowdens-first-emails-to-poitras/.

ENDNOTES

179   Maass, Peter. "How Laura Poitras Helped Snowden Spill His Secrets." *New York Times*, August 13, 2013, sec. Magazine. https://www.nytimes. com/2013/08/18/magazine/laura-poitras-snowden.html.

180   Snowden, Edward. "Biggest Leak in the History of Data Journalism Just Went Live, and It's about Corruption. Http://Panamapapers.Sueddeutsche. de/En/ Pic.Twitter.Com/638aIu8oSU." Tweet. @Snowden, April 3, 2016. https://twitter.com/Snowden/status/716683740903247873.

181   Obermayer, Bastian, and Frederik Obermaier. *The Panama Papers: Breaking the Story of How the Rich and Powerful Hide Their Money*. Revised edition. London: Oneworld Publications, 2017.

182   Testa, Jessica. "A Handy Guide To The Very Fake Twitter Accounts Of Glenn Greenwald And Edward Snowden." BuzzFeed News, June 12, 2013. https:// www.buzzfeednews.com/article/jtes/a-handy-guide-to-the-very-fake- twitter-accounts-of-glenn-gre.

183   Greenberg, Andy. "How Reporters Pulled Off the Panama Papers, the Biggest Leak in Whistleblower History." Wired, April 4, 2016. https://www. wired.com/2016/04/reporters-pulled-off-panama-papers-biggest-leak- whistleblower-history/.

184   Manning, Chelsea. "Statement in Support of Providence Inquiry -- U.S. v Private First Class (PFC) Bradley E. Manning (U)," March 11, 2013. https:// www.armycourtmartialdefense.com/2013/03/pfc-bradley-mannings- statement.html.

185   Corbett, Rachel. "Court Dismisses Former Artforum Employee Amanda Schmitt's Lawsuits Against the Magazine and Knight Landesman." artnet News, January 3, 2019. https://news.artnet.com/art-world/amanda-schmitt- artforum-dismissal-1431397.

186   Schmitt v Artforum Intl. Mag., Inc., No. 159496/2017 (Supreme Court, New York County December 20, 2018). https://law.justia.com/cases/new-york/ other-courts/2018/2018-ny-slip-op-33345-u.html.

187   Marczak, Bill, John Scott-Railton, Sarah McKune, Bahr Abdul Razzak, and Ron Deibert. "Hide and Seek: Tracking NSO Group's Pegasus Spyware to Operations in 45 Countries." The Citizen Lab, September 18, 2018. https:// citizenlab.ca/2018/09/hide-and-seek-tracking-nso-groups-pegasus-spyware- to-operations-in-45-countries/.

188   Scott-Railton, John, Bill Marczak, Siena Anstis, Bahr Abdul Razzak, Masashi Crete-Nishihata, and Ron Deibert. "Reckless VI: Mexican Journalists Investigating Cartels Targeted with NSO Spyware Following Assassination of Colleague." The Citizen Lab, November 27, 2018. https://citizenlab.

ca/2018/11/mexican-journalists-investigating-cartels-targeted-nso-spyware-following-assassination-colleague/.

189   Melendez, Steven. "Manafort Allegedly Used 'Foldering' to Hide Emails. Here's How It Works." Fast Company, June 15, 2018. https://www.fastcompany.com/40586130/manafort-allegedly-used-foldering-to-hide-emails-heres-how-it-works.

190   Cardozo, Nate, Gennie Gebhart, and Erica Portnoy. "Secure Messaging? More Like A Secure Mess." Electronic Frontier Foundation, March 26, 2018. https://www.eff.org/deeplinks/2018/03/secure-messaging-more-secure-mess.

191   Seitz, Justin. "How To Blow Your Online Cover With URL Previews." Bellingcat, January 4, 2019. https://www.bellingcat.com/resources/how-tos/2019/01/04/how-to-blow-your-online-cover-with-url-previews/.

192   Zetter, Kim. "Turns Out Police Stingray Spy Tools Can Indeed Record Calls." Wired, October 28, 2015. https://www.wired.com/2015/10/stingray-government-spy-tools-can-record-calls-new-documents-confirm/.

193   Greenwald, Glenn. "NSA Collecting Phone Records of Millions of Verizon Customers Daily." The Guardian, June 6, 2013, sec. US news. https://www.theguardian.com/world/2013/jun/06/nsa-phone-records-verizon-court-order.

194   Bohm, Allie. "How Long Is Your Cell Phone Company Hanging On To Your Data?" American Civil Liberties Union, September 28, 2011. https://www.aclu.org/blog/national-security/how-long-your-cell-phone-company-hanging-your-data.

195   Scahill, Jeremy, and Josh Begley. "How Spies Stole the Keys to the Encryption Castle." The Intercept, February 19, 2015. https://theintercept.com/2015/02/19/great-sim-heist/.

196   "Security & Privacy · Wire." Accessed August 27, 2019. https://wire.com/en/security/.

197   Seitz, Justin. "How To Blow Your Online Cover With URL Previews." Bellingcat, January 4, 2019. https://www.bellingcat.com/resources/how-tos/2019/01/04/how-to-blow-your-online-cover-with-url-previews/.

198   "Grand Jury Subpoena for Signal User Data, Eastern District of Virginia." Signal, October 4, 2016. https://signal.org/bigbrother/eastern-virginia-grand-jury/.

199   "OnionShare." Accessed August 27, 2019. https://onionshare.org.

200   Morelle, Rebecca. "The Hum That Helps to Fight Crime." BBC News, December 12, 2012, sec. Science & Environment. https://www.bbc.com/news/science-environment-20629671.

201 Rice, Andrew. "Daniel Ellsberg Is Still Thinking About the Papers He Didn't Get to Leak." Intelligencer, November 28, 2017. http://nymag.com/intelligencer/2017/11/daniel-ellsberg-on-the-doomsday-machine.html.

202 Ruiz, Rebecca R. "Olympic Doping Diaries: Chemist's Notes Bolster Case Against Russia." New York Times, November 28, 2017, sec. Sports. https://www.nytimes.com/2017/11/28/sports/olympics/russia-doping.html.

203 Sidman, Jessica, and Anna Spiegel. "The Inside Story of Mike Isabella's Fallen Empire." Washingtonian, November 26, 2018. https://www.washingtonian.com/2018/11/26/the-inside-story-of-mike-isabellas-fallen-empire/.

204 "Hollow Nickel/Rudolf Abel." Page. Federal Bureau of Investigation. Accessed August 27, 2019. https://www.fbi.gov/history/famous-cases/hollow-nickel-rudolph-abel.

205 Ibrahim, Mukhtar M. "Minneapolis FBI Agent Charged with Leaking Classified Information to Reporter." MPR News, March 28, 2018. https://www.mprnews.org/story/2018/03/28/minneapolis-fbi-agent-charged-with-leaking-classified-information.

206 Honan, Mat. "Oops! Did Vice Just Give Away John McAfee's Location With Photo Metadata?" Wired, December 3, 2012. https://www.wired.com/2012/12/oops-did-vice-just-give-away-john-mcafees-location-with-this-photo/.

207 "Distributing Word Documents with a Locating Beacon." SecuriTeam (blog), August 30, 2000. https://securiteam.com/securitynews/5cp13002aa/.

208 "Criminal Complaint, Case 1:17-MJ-024, Document 5," June 5, 2017. https://www.documentcloud.org/documents/3772218-Reality-Winner-Complaint.html.

209 So, Hemmy. "Whistle-Blower or Thief in Diebold Case?" Los Angeles Times, March 18, 2006. https://www.latimes.com/archives/la-xpm-2006-mar-18-me-heller18-story.html.

210 Benner, Katie. "A Nuclear Site Guard Accused Colleagues of Sexual Assault. Then She Was Fired." New York Times, January 25, 2019, sec. U.S. https://www.nytimes.com/2019/01/25/us/politics/department-of-energy-sexual-assault.html.

211 "Jennifer Glover Disciplinary Decision Letter," New York Times, November 7, 2018. https://int.nyt.com/data/documenthelper/581-soc-letter-glover-assault/d25ccd81035d1ea32e59/optimized/full.pdf.

212 McDonaugh, Jane. "How to Completely Erase a Fingerprint on Document Paper." Legal Beagle, June 5, 2017. https://legalbeagle.com/8468877-completely-erase-fingerprint-document-paper.html.

213 Marr, Bernard. "How Blockchain Will Transform The Supply Chain And Logistics Industry." *Forbes*. Accessed August 27, 2019. https://www.forbes.com/sites/bernardmarr/2018/03/23/how-blockchain-will-transform-the-supply-chain-and-logistics-industry/.

214 Schneier, Bruce. "PDF Redacting Failure." Schneier on Security, May 3, 2005. https://www.schneier.com/blog/archives/2005/05/pdf_radacting_f.html.

215 First Look Media. "PDF Redact Tools," August 21, 2019. https://github.com/firstlookmedia/pdf-redact-tools.

216 "Removing Personal Information from MP3s Bought on Amazon." aaronk, April 6, 2017. https://aaronk.me/removing-personal-information-from-mp3s-bought-off-amazon/.

217 "MAT: Metadata Anonymisation Toolkit." Accessed January 20, 2018. https://mat.boum.org/.

218 jvoisin. "Mat2." GitLab. Accessed August 27, 2019. https://0xacab.org/jvoisin/mat2.

219 Rice, Andrew. "Daniel Ellsberg Is Still Thinking About the Papers He Didn't Get to Leak." Intelligencer, November 28, 2017. http://nymag.com/intelligencer/2017/11/daniel-ellsberg-on-the-doomsday-machine.html.

220 Fuller, Adam D., Elizabeth Shively Boatwright, and Bryan E. Meek. "No Attorney-Client Privilege for You: The Crime-Fraud Exception," April 8, 2014. https://www.americanbar.org/groups/litigation/committees/trial-practice/articles/2014/spring2014-0414-crime-fraud-exception-attorney-client-privilege/.

221 Rosenzweig, Paul. "Michael Cohen, the Attorney-Client Privilege, and the Crime-Fraud Exception." Brookings, April 10, 2018. https://www.brookings.edu/blog/fixgov/2018/04/10/michael-cohen-the-attorney-client-privilege-and-the-crime-fraud-exception/.

222 Cimpanu, Catalin. "Researcher Wants to Protect Whistleblowers Against Hidden Printer Dots." Bleeping Computer, June 9, 2017. https://www.bleepingcomputer.com/news/security/researcher-wants-to-protect-whistleblowers-against-hidden-printer-dots/.

223 Kopplin, Zack. "How the FBI Uses the Freedom of Information Act to Track down Whistleblowers." *Washington Post*, April 9, 2018, sec. Perspective. https://www.washingtonpost.com/news/posteverything/wp/2018/04/09/how-the-fbi-uses-the-freedom-of-information-act-to-track-down-whistleblowers/.

Acknowledgements

It turns out that writing a book was among the hardest things I've attempted in my life thus far. In retrospect, a first book takes a lot of naïveté, and I have been humbled by the writing process. I now have a tremendous amount of respect for anyone who publishes a book. In this journey, I had many to support me, and only through their input and help was this book possible.

I must start with my publisher, OR Books, and in particular John Oakes, who took a chance on me. Tim Harper did the first edit of the book and coached me through the process, encouraging me at times and being the task master at others. His experience with the written word and how to get the best out of a writer was invaluable. Margaret Schneider sat next to me "in virtual" for months. Together we honed sentences, researched details and strategies, and discussed all of the edge cases—this book would not have been possible without her brilliant brain. Likewise, Daniel Chaffee and I spent hours thinking through the issues and arguments, figuring out the best way to structure the book and make the content accessible.

My thinking and mindset for this book were only possible after years of creating projects, teaching, and collaborating with others interested in privacy and security. This includes my close collaboration with Taze and Noname at LA Cryptoparty. Together we have figured out new ways of teaching privacy and security. This was the setup I needed to write this book. Christopher Kardambikis, Don Russell, and Provisions Library supported and fostered the initial idea of this project. Owen Mundy has been a longtime collaborator on privacy and security projects, and I wouldn't be thinking of these things today without his influence.

The recommendations in this book and particular sections were reviewed by the expertise of Tom Devine, David Huerta, and Chris Walker—thank you all not only for your help on this book, but also for your years of fighting the right fight. This gratitude extends to the community that is building technology to support privacy and security and the journalists and legal experts who are supporting whistleblowers. Many were gracious enough to be interviewed by me for this book, and I thank you all for your thoughts and opinions.

I had no idea ahead of time that I would spend holidays, mornings before work, and weekends writing. Thank you to my partner, Mariona; my family; my friends; and my colleagues at Alley, who were ever supportive over these years. I hope I have the chance to support you all as you've supported me.

Finally, thank you to all of you who have decided to stand up and use your voice when you see something wrong. You are the inspiration for this book. I hope that this book can give back a fraction of what you all have given to the world. Thank you.